Praise for *Shotgun Rider*

For over forty years, I have been a Shotgun Rider, that is, an associate pastor working alongside the Senior Pastor. There are thousands of shotgun riders, serving in churches around the world. They bear different labels, but they are not the senior leader; they don't make the final decisions. I have never read anything more helpful than Doug Brown's book, *Shotgun Rider: Restoring Your Passion for the Ministry Trail*. It is written specifically to pastoral leaders who are on the team but are not senior pastors. I highly recommend it.

GARY CHAPMAN, PHD, AUTHOR OF *THE FIVE LOVE LANGUAGES*

My friend Doug Brown has written a must-read book for anyone working on staff in ministry. *Shotgun Rider* will challenge you to embrace the significance of your role and to keep your heart in the right place in spite of your circumstances. A much-needed book, written by someone who has succeeded at living out these principles.

MARK JOBE, LEAD PASTOR OF NEW LIFE COMMUNITY CHURCH,
CHICAGO; AUTHOR OF *UNSTUCK: OUT OF YOUR CAVE INTO YOUR CALL*

Doug Brown has written a little book that packs a big punch. *Shotgun Rider* is crammed full of great stories, insight, and wisdom that will benefit veteran and rookie ministry workers alike. With *Shotgun Rider*, Brown has given a wonderful gift to the ministry leadership community. I found myself rereading most sections because they are all packed with so much good stuff. Share the word: *Shotgun Rider* is a GREAT read!

KURT JOHNSTON, PASTOR TO STUDENTS, SADDLEBACK CHURCH

D1606410

Shotgun Rider

SHOTGUN RIDER

RESTORING YOUR PASSION FOR
THE MINISTRY TRAIL

K. DOUGLAS BROWN

Deep River
B O O K S

To Juliana,
The love of my life:
I'd do it all again with you in a heartbeat.

Acknowledgments

I'm grateful for godly parents and in-laws: Ken and Jan Brown and Lee and Carol Carson. The strength of your faith and your prayers are realized in our lives every day.

I'm thankful each day for the four greatest gifts a parent could ever be given: Kohley, Carson, Andrew, and Ivy.

Thank you, Luann Yarrow Doman, Dean Kautzmann, and Douglas Stepelton, for giving me the chance to reignite a passion for writing.

Special thanks to Jenni Burke and Kelsi Shelton at D.C. Jacobson and Associates for your guidance and for encouraging me forward.

Thank you, Dan Balow at the Steve Laube Agency, for believing in me and not requiring me to dress up for our "dates."

I'm grateful daily for my peers, the shotgun riders at Metropolitan: Rick Hermansen, Trudy Hoffsommer, Casey Oliver, Matt Menhennett, and John Strauss. You guys make showing up fun. Thank you, Randy Faulkner, for giving me the freedom to follow my calling.

Thanks to those who encouraged me in my writing along the way: Bobby Gupta, Mark Hitchcock, Tim Kimmel, Michael Lawson, Don Miller, Patrick O'Connor, Bill Puckett, Greg Smalley, Scott Way, David Wyrtzen, and Wes Yoder.

I'm thankful for the insightful attention to detail and hours spent reworking this manuscript by Rachel Starr Thomson, and for the great cover work by Andy Carmichael. From the start, your *let's get this right* attitude shone through.

I'm deeply grateful to Bill Carmichael, Kit Tosello, and the folks at Deep River Books for seeing the potential of this work. I'm honored beyond belief to be chosen as first-place winner of the 2014 Deep River Books writing contest.

"He says, "Be still and know that I am God."

PSALM 46:10

CONTENTS

FOREWORD

You're about to have a conversation with my friend Doug.

Much of what you are about to encounter is real, right from his life, and yet, if you're in ministry, it probably describes the journey you are on… or heading toward. *Shotgun Rider* comes from the place where life and Scripture meet, and wisdom is born.

Quick story…This actually happened.

I landed a new position at a large church. A number of pastors reported to me and were "on my team." Where would I start? How would I assess the team? Everyone was busy (That's good, right?). You could feel their latent stress over the big program, the big new church building, and their big dreams. It's the unspoken mess that church staffs rarely speak about.

So here was one of my first questions to staff: Do you see yourself as a leader or a pastor? To my surprise, they all answered the same, without reservation. Leader! The thinking is this: Leaders start movements = used by God to do big things, while pastors huddle with people and have small vision and capacity. I admit, the terms I just used are loaded, and the meanings shift. But the point is that it's easy to fall into thinking our value and calling are tied to our job description.

This is why I love the following chapters. Doug Brown speaks to the sacred calling so many of us have responded to, and how often we must fight to fulfill it in many of the places where we serve. You won't find exaggerated pulpit stories here. Doug speaks to pastors as real people, with conflicting gravitational pulls. Because he has plenty of his own frustrations, fears, and battle wounds, you'll find him a trusted confidant.

To those of us who are at a ministry or career crossroads, Doug speaks pragmatically. Would it be better to leave my current position? What do I do when leadership isn't leading? How do I, in a Jesus-honoring way, navigate churches that are wrangled with politics? Sure enough, Doug has been there too. Without bitterness, but rather with charm, vulnerability, and open confession, he describes your current reality through story and lays out pathways that will allow God to lead though times of organizational chaos or outright failure.

You will not get through this book without coming face-to-face with your true motivation and calling, which has the potential to be both frightening and encouraging simultaneously. The book flushes out like a formidable river any false guides that have been shadowing your ministry "career."

So here is my encouragement to you before you go on this little jaunt with Doug as a tour guide. Open your heart and hands to heaven, and ask Jesus to show you what really motivates you. What is your true calling? What's the why behind the things that frustrate you? Who are you trying to impress?

The lightning that will strike from this read is not in a new program or strategy toward your church or staff. More beneficial is when God allows lightning to strike the core of your identity and calling. This is where passion is restored.

The most important part of *Shotgun Rider* is what you bring to it. If you are looking for a best-practices resource, you'll find some of that, but you'll miss out. If you're hoping this book will motivate your staff to "get on board," you might want to read it again.

Doug Brown has written this book from a place of devotional honesty. If you take the same approach, the words and stories will jump off the page. The book comes from a place of significant clarity and love for the Father's true calling in our lives. If you recognize your own need for perspective and encouragement, you're holding the right book.

So before you turn the page, do this one thing...

Place this book aside for a moment and get on your knees. (Okay, that's two things). *Shotgun Rider* will become amazingly loud and maybe a little scary when you do. Yee haw!

ERIC VENABLE

CITY DIRECTOR FOR CITY TEAM MINISTRIES

SAN FRANCISCO BAY AREA, CALIFORNIA

INTRODUCTION

One Wednesday deep into the fall, I found myself waiting in the car with the engine already running. It was the start of our usual midweek routine, our harried race out the door for our church's weekly youth and children's programs. I would take the kids, and my wife, Juli, would meet up with us later at the church. The kids and I would grab a pizza on the way over, to be inhaled in my office before we all headed to our respective programs or Bible studies. I had the two younger ones already strapped in, and with a watchful eye to the clock on the dash, I made regular checks over my shoulder for the older two to come through the garage and onto the driveway.

With a burst of noise I heard them coming, bantering in quick tempo.

"I call shotty."

"No, I get shotgun, you had it last time."

I could feel the escalation.

"You always sit up front."

"Too bad, I called it first!" They wrestled over the door handle. I quickly settled the dispute with one statement: "Tell me who rode up front last time!"

As they slumped into their places, I looked over at the preteen wonder next to me, and it hit me like a pallet of bricks. This is me, I thought. I'm the one riding shotgun. I'm not the senior pastor, the driver, the one holding the reins. I'm riding shotgun, and I'm okay with it. I've had this front-seat view of God's work for over two decades now, and every bit of it's been an adventure. I love my spot, and I'd fight to keep it.

Her interruption shook me from my half-daydream. "Dad, don't we need to go?" I navigated myself back into Wednesday mode, and as we drove away, I thought about the privilege and the fun of following God all these years. It's been quite a ride, and I'd do it again in a heartbeat.

Let's be real about it, though. Working at a church has its own set of challenges. When a new staff position would open, somewhere along the way one of the applicants would almost certainly say, "I just think it would be so encouraging to work at the church and be a part of what God is doing." At this point sirens and whistles would go off in my head: WARN-ING, WARNING! I've seen it numerous times. Soon after beginning their work, I know what will happen. They will be hit with the realization that pastors are human. They will realize that parishioners are human and that ministry can be downright discouraging at times if you're not spiritually prepared.

It isn't always roses working at a church. How could it be? After all, you're on the front line of a raging battle. Moreover, many of the challenges are unique to being in the non-lead role:

- You're the one who's supposed to recruit all the volunteers for the programs and great ideas that someone else up the chain thinks up.
- At times you feel you have no avenue to voice your concerns because you don't hold any power.
- You've been asked, "When are you going to become a real pas-tor?"
- You feel like you're so far down the line that no one cares what you think or even knows that you exist.
- Someone else doles out your workload, perhaps without sen-sitivity to your ability to get it all done inside of fifty hours.
- Your creative ideas for improvements don't get taken seriously by decision makers.
- You are required to attend board or council meetings at which you have no vote.
- Working with children or youth, you rarely or never get to address the people in "Big Church."
- You work hard to make a program or event happen but some-one else gets to tell about it from the platform Sunday morning and your name is never mentioned.

No, it hasn't been easy. Ministry is hard, and being number two—or number thirty-two or maybe number one hundred and thirty-two—is a special challenge. But on the way over to the church that evening, I thought about so many people in the churches where I'd served. What a privilege to have a part in their walk with Christ and to see them grow! I remembered kids who came to Christ in each of our youth groups. I thought about some who came through our ministries and went on to serve on the mission field or the pastorate or other places of service. I reminded myself of several who serve in government positions, trying to make a difference, and about those who have served in the military and even given their lives for our country. I thought about many who are now leaders in their own churches and communities.

Then my mind flooded with all the trips and experiences through the years, things I'd since forgotten about. Youth retreats by the seaside and summer camps in 115-degree heat; snow camps and all-night parties on New Year's Eve. Weeklong ski trips and hiking trips on the Continental Divide and Appalachian Trails. Nights spent under the stars on camping trips and the time we spent several hours in a broken-down bus in a blizzard. There was the time I saw our loaded trailer pass us by on the shoulder of the road and the several hours we spent trying to retrieve it from the ditch. I thought of fifth-quarter outreaches after high school football games where our students led their friends to Christ.

Then the flood became overwhelming with the swelling tide of mission-trip memories. My mind went to places like Eluru, Cholula, Manoguayabo, and Las Caobus, places where our teens got to see God's hand at work in miraculous ways. I remembered the fear I felt while looking down the barrel of a hostile policeman's AK-47 and wishing I knew the Creole word for "Please" while he and his comrades robbed us. There was the night we spent in prayer listening to the pulsing beat of voodoo drums, and the evening in India when we fled a church service as a band of Hindu zealots showed up with clubs. I recalled clutching my soaking bags on the back of an open train car in a jungle monsoon, wishing we had a ticket to ride inside. I remembered how God answered our prayer, and how we were able to finish the trip in the dry sleeper car.

Most cherished of all these memories was the great privilege of preaching under a thatched roof in a remote tribal village in Asia. As long as I live, I will never forget them informing me afterward that they had been praying for ten years for a foreigner to come and preach the gospel in their humble church—ten years! All I could do was stand there sobbing, realizing that it was me who was the answered prayer. I was once just an ordinary kid on the streets of a Chicago suburb. How did I get selected for this call? How could I be their answer? Oh, how I wanted to preach that message over—how I wanted someone else to be their answered prayer! I left feeling I'd received much more from them than I'd left behind. What a great honor to experience the hand of God at work around the world and to escort our students into these endeavors. What a rich life I've been privileged to have, and I'm so glad I chose to take that step of faith so many years back.

Maybe these aren't your own ministry experiences, but I'm sure you could name yours: the experiences you cherish, the rewarding opportunities that make you glad you're on the trail. Though being in professional ministry doesn't make anyone more spiritual or a better Christian than anyone else, there are specific experiences and yes, certain rewards, that are unique to those in ministry. You just don't have those encounters if you're not sitting in the front seat. In the shotgun position, you are given a gift: a close-up view of God's work in people's lives.

My Wednesday epiphany came at a point when I'm usually at a lower emotional ebb. I've come to recognize seasonal ups and downs, and late fall is usually a valley for me. There's something about that time of year that brings me down emotionally and spiritually. The excitement of the beginning of the school year and all the ministry activity that began with it is overshadowed by the dulling routine, and it's usually about this time that I begin to hear from leaders who are discouraged in their service. The approach of winter and the accompanying lull in attendance, paired with the challenge of keeping volunteers satisfied at their posts, seem to be in cahoots to create a slurry of ministry blues.

I've been through some pretty difficult times in ministry, including a sexual scandal involving a youth leader and some students, a leadership implosion, an unintended eighteen-month sabbatical, and several staff members who tried unsuccessfully to get me fired. Still, taking all this into consideration, I'd do it again. The joys and the victories far exceed the failures and difficulties. It's been a great life—it *is* a great life—and I can't wait to see what the next half holds.

We've all experienced it—that moment when we realized how hard this was going to be and had to look the beast square in the eyes and wrestle it to the ground or get out. If you're reading this, I'll surmise that you're a lifer, a survivor at least to this point. You've made it through the fire so far and you're still clipping along, perhaps a little jaded but still nostalgic about your early days in ministry. It's my goal to help you find your way back, to help you rediscover your love for the ride. I aim to help you thrive, not just survive. You can once again feel the excitement of being number two, and I want to help you get it back. For you, my friend, are the shotgun rider!

CHAPTER ONE

THE SHOTGUN RIDER

In the days before bungee jumping and skydiving, before spelunking and rock climbing, there was the high-riding shotgun rider. Equipped with adrenaline and fearless determination, these high-stakes riders found just the task to match their grit and dauntless courage: it was theirs to ride alongside the stagecoach driver with a shotgun in their laps, eyes out for predators and bandits alike. They protected cargo and passengers and kept the driver able to do his job in the face of many dangers. These were the days before Kevlar and bulletproof glass, before shock absorbers and pavement, and the shotgun spot was no place for cowards or weak-kneed sissies. The work was hazardous—life threatening—and the rides were less than comfortable.

Interestingly, the label "shotgun rider" didn't even exist in those days. No one really knows where the term originated—we may have western-themed movies to thank. Today we honor the position and attach a mystique to the riders. In those days it was just your job, and you endured the troubles for the adventure and what little pay was offered.

Those souls brave enough for the task knew the rewards of the adventure would amply repay those fit enough to endure. And so it is in ministry. Today, a high percentage of ministry roles are filled by those who are not the senior pastor. These positions are hazardous—and rewarding. If you've found yourself in the shotgun seat, get strapped in. You will need courage and determination; you will need endurance and raw grit; your spot is not for the faint of heart. More than what you are able to draw from within, know that you have God working on your behalf. No shotgun rider rides alone. Remember that in that same passage of Scripture where we are called to make disciples, our Lord promises to be with us until the end of the age. The God who called you is at work building his church, and you are a key part of that work.

The shotgun rider is paramount to the success of the church today. Does that sentence strike you as unexpected? Chances are you feel at least a little powerless at times—perhaps most of the time—and you wonder if you're making any difference at all. You've brought your ideas to your staff, to church board meetings or team strategy sessions, and you feel like you're not being heard. Meanwhile, those up the chain of church politics seem to get their own agenda items approved on the spot. Churches have a way of bypassing their own leadership structures at times, and often it's the shotgun riders who get chewed up in the process.

This book is for you if you play a secondary role in your church or ministry. Whether you find yourself in a supportive pastoral position or you serve in worship ministries; whether you're in children's or youth ministry or you serve in missions or a parachurch organization; you will face many unique challenges from your vantage point in a variety of secondary responsibilities.

But no matter the challenges you face, hear this clearly: You are in a place of important work, and your vision and your ministry matter greatly. God has placed you in your spot not to take orders and get pushed around (even though this probably happens some). Rather, God has called you to be a person of leadership and vision. That might mean losing the battle over your list but winning the war over the people's minds and hearts. There are greater issues in the church than what to do with a few extra dollars or what color the carpet should be. At times your position will require you to herald a call for change. It means sometimes standing before the people with a warning, as some of Israel's greatest prophets did. At other times, you may find yourself helping to create an atmosphere of teamwork and peace.

In many ways, you play a role in the church today that is new on the scene. Just as the stagecoach changed the way people and goods traveled, and therefore necessitated a new class of men to help guard and guide them, so your place in the ministry of the local church may be the product of recent changes to church culture and structure.

THE NEW LANDSCAPE

After twenty-five years of ministry to youth and children and their families, I find myself between two churches: the one that was familiar to my parents and the church that is sprouting up as we speak. I was born in the last month of the last year of the baby boom. Many of you will have no idea what that means, so understand this: It means that technically, I fit into the previous generation. However, I *feel* much more at home with you, those who followed the boomers, the GenXers and the Millennials. Culturally, I'm more like you than I am like my parents and their parents.

I say this only to make the point that as I was growing up, I saw the beginnings of the disappearance of the great culture. When I use the term "great," what I mean is that it was a large and potent force both in number and in what it stood for. It was great too because of the huge strides it accomplished in the world. Our forefathers, the builders and boomers, were responsible for the defeat of Hitler and the collapse of communism. They gave us penicillin and satellites, making possible Google and cell phones. We owe a lot to them.

What I observed as I grew up, be it good or bad, was that the previous generations were much more homogeneous than ours. In other words, my parents' culture was much more like the culture of their parents and so on. The church they knew was also much more like that of the church of their parents. In fact, the church didn't change much at all in the generations previous to ours. That's not all bad, and it's not all good; it just is. Today's culture, however, is not much like anything before it. It's a new landscape.

In some ways I feel a little like one of those movie characters who get knocked on the head, go into the hospital, and wake up a couple of decades later realizing everything has changed. One day a few years back it hit me: Everything's different now. Everything is different, and I like it. Because of the time in which I was born, I got to see and be a part of this metamorphosis—one that has taken place incredibly fast. As the staid models, the old tried-and-somewhat-true forms fade away, I see many exciting changes on the horizon. Much of what I see is refreshing and vibrant, and it gives me great hope for the church my children will inherit.

One of the most energizing elements is the rising host of shotgun riders appearing on the scene. You see, in the church of my parents, there was the pastor. "Solo pastor" wasn't even a needed term. Of course he was a solo pastor; they all were! If there was a second pastor type on the scene, he was usually in training and preparing to lead a church of his own somewhere else.

The scene is very different now, as can be vividly illustrated by the conferences available for ministers. When I first began my ministry as a professional youth pastor, the thought of a conference for youth pastors was a cutting-edge idea. My first pastors' conference had breakout sessions for youth pastors, and this was a new concept then. The atmosphere in those sessions was electric. At the time, even the term "youth pastor" was relatively new, so to think that these pioneers could get together in the same room and find support and encouragement was exhilarating. Back then I could name every youth guy in my denomination's seven-state region, and most of the others scattered across the nation. Today I can hardly count the youth pastors in that same region, much less name them.

And that's only one position. Now there are a host of conferences for a plethora of ministry positions. There are conferences for church administrators and executive pastors. There are children's pastors' conferences, conferences for those in pastoral counseling, and conferences for the leaders of singles ministries and for those who minister to the divorced. I once saw an advertisement for a youth pastors' conference that looked interesting. I wanted to sign up to attend, but then I noticed in the brochure that the conference was only open to those whose churches had an attendance between 2500 and 5000. It's mind-boggling to think how things have changed.

There's a new wave of young pastors and church staff members on the scene, and there are legions of them across the nation and around the world. It is to you I write: this new generation of pastors, ministers, directors, team leaders, and volunteers. My concern is for you and all those who, though they are not holding the reins of control in the church, are bringing about the dawn of a new day and are in for the ride of their lives.

As I'm certain you've already learned, all of this change is not without difficulty. The new breed carries with them hurts and burdens that are also new. The role of the #2 or #3 or #123 staffer is full of challenges. Many staff environments are characterized by great teamwork, but challenges abound nonetheless. Too often you've worked behind the scenes with little credit or recognition. You have little pulpit exposure, little opportunity to be up front where accolades run thick and opportunities for horn tooting come easily. And your work too often goes unnoticed by those up the chain. I've sat through enough meetings and gatherings of non–senior pastor types to know the stakes are high and the need for encouragement great.

I once worked on a staff with a guy we'll call Joseph. He was a little hard to take, a tad brash, a bit of a bullhorn. In the stories he loved to tell, he was almost always the hero. One day I spent most of a morning working on a project. One of the elements of the project involved some hurdles in the department over which he was the head. I spent over an hour carving out a solution with a person from his department. Later that afternoon as I was about to put a wrap on it, Joseph popped his head into my office. The point of his visit was to tell me that he had worked out a fix on a problem he had uncovered—the problem which we had already worked out. The plan he presented was our plan. Apparently he had been briefed on the situation without being told who had worked it all out, and now he was taking credit for our work.

I could feel anger welling up inside of me. If I were a cartoon character, there would have been steam shooting out of my ears. I couldn't even think of an appropriate response. To say "thank you" would have seemed dishonest. "I appreciate what you've done" wouldn't be true either, and it would have been a slap in the face of his assistant, who was the real mastermind. I just said, "I'm glad it's all been worked out."

I understand! I've sat in your conference rooms and heard your stories of poor treatment and political dealings. I've been in those denominational meetings where tales of less than godly staff relations are told. I've walked in your steps, I've sat in your meetings, and I've heard your stories of unappreciated, unrewarded ministry. My point is not to create an avenue for another gripe session, but to say I get it because I've been there too. But my message is this: You can get through it, yes, you can *thrive,* and the thriving doesn't depend on your surroundings as much as you might think. I have great hope for this generation of ministers—for you, the shotgun riders. I believe you and your peers will rise to the challenges of this new era.

A New Attitude

What words come to mind when you think of your position and stature at your church? Do words like *berated, undervalued, unappreciated,* or *insignificant* rise to the fore? If so, you're not alone. Many church workers report feeling unappreciated and overlooked in their ministry.

I remember when I was wrestling with whether or not to choose a career in ministry. I felt like God was pushing me in that direction but worried about how a ministry career was going to help me pay the bills. That was nearly thirty years ago, and I can chuckle about it now, but at the time I only knew I didn't want to be poor the rest of my life, and I'd seen too many pastor and missionary types who were. One night in a watershed moment, I surrendered and told God I would do whatever he wanted me to do, even if it meant I'd be poor the rest of my life. I entered the ministry fully prepared to live in a lower income bracket. What I *wasn't* prepared for was how often in ministry you live with a lack of appreciation. Appreciation doesn't put bread on the table, but it sure makes it a lot more fun to serve!

Ministry is hard. I have told my own children that if there's any other career path they might choose, they should consider it, and only if they were absolutely sure God was leading them into ministry should they take that path. You'll face long hours, difficult personalities, and the never-ending challenge of finding funds for all the ideas and ministries you oversee. And for many, there is the expectation that you will live in a glass house as you work out these challenges.

Every shotgun rider faces demons of a more personal nature too. One of the greatest discontents can happen when you begin to wish you were the senior pastor or maybe the pastor or staffer one level up. Many have gone into ministry intending to climb the ladder. Too many have looked at their current spot as a stepping stone to somewhere else. My message to you here is simple: Don't do that. Be satisfied to serve where you have been planted. Let God be the one who promotes you, not because you played golf with the right person or went to all the right functions but because you were noted as a good leader with a pure heart and a deep desire to serve.

I get it. Before I was moved into my current role as pastor of family ministries, I was the children's pastor. From a human point of view, there is no more lowly position on any church staff. In terms of a church ladder of success, the children's pastor falls somewhere below the youth pastor and perhaps just above the janitor, though often these two are seen working together. When you're the children's pastor, you're the last on the pulpit fill list, and you're usually only asked to be on the platform when the youth guy is sick or out of town. You don't last long without some level of humility. Personally, I never cared about titles—I knew I was serving where God wanted me, and I knew he had given me the gifts and abilities to do it. Sometimes, though, it's only human to wish your name could be listed a little closer to the top of the staff page.

For the record, I didn't go looking to be the family pastor; I sort of fell into it. I'd been dabbling all along in family ministry activities: a parenting conference, a marriage enrichment weekend, parent and family counseling, and Bible studies for men. One afternoon I was on a conference call with George Hillman at my seminary. He was my professor for an internship course I was taking at the time. John Strauss, my overseer at the church, had been serving as my on-site advisor and was on the call with me in my office. At one point in the conversation George said to John, "John, we've been looking at Doug's giftedness and his leadership abilities, and we've studied his background and passions, and it's my recommendation that you move him into a family ministries role at the church." I about fell off my chair, but that was the beginning of my transition into family ministry.

I'll be honest: though I thoroughly enjoy what I do, it's not like some great dignity comes along with the new name plate on my door. All it means is the church changed my title to include some of the things I'd already been doing and added a few more. Sometimes fancy titles are just a way of saying "You can do this work too."

After the conference call that day, I went home and told my wife I was one step closer to my plan of world domination. It's always good not to take yourself too seriously, and anyway, when we get to heaven I don't think we're going to be lined up in any sort of staff pecking order. The janitor may just be the line leader! Titles only mean anything on this side, and I'm pretty sure the Bible still says something about the first being last and God choosing the weak things so he can confound the wise (1 Corinthians 1:27).

It's important that our attitude line up with that reality—the truth about position in the kingdom of God. Please make sure you get this. In God's economy your work is vital, no matter what your your title is or what others think. There is no more important role than to work with children and assist in ushering them into God's kingdom. There is no place closer to the front line than to serve in the youth group and speak to young people about vital issues like their walk with God or how to avoid temptation. These are the places where you get to see lives influenced in a great way. So many decisions are made during these formative years—in the youth rooms and at kids' camps and during Vacation Bible School. And while we're at it, you can be sure there is no more important role than leading God's people in praising him each week as they're ushered into the presence of the Lord in worship. There is nothing more thrilling than to direct women's ministry and to lead women in the study of God's Word. There is no more necessary place than to pastor the singles, or the seniors, or the small groups. One and all, the shotgun riders are in the thick of the fray.

While it's certainly not a lesser role to be the senior pastor, those in that role are involved in many things related to the business of the church. Senior pastors don't get to help shape the lives of children and youth or women, at least not on a weekly basis and certainly not at the level we do. Senior pastors don't generally get to specialize in one area or with one age. For the most part they are generalists, not specialists. If you've been called to pastor at the senior level, then by all means get your education and your training and go do it. But if not, or not yet, then settle in with your calling and your role and find joy in what you've been called and prepared to do.

You are in a position of influence in your church, and you can accomplish great things from where you are. The things that ultimately define a church have little to do with what's said from the pulpit or from the platform on Sunday morning. The things that define a church, that define *your* church, happen in a thousand little interchanges right in your area. They happen in the back hallways, in the kitchen, in the nursery, and in the youth room. How you handle yourself and your responsibilities is noticed by God even if it isn't noticed by anyone else. The challenge is to carry yourself in a way that is honoring to him. You, my friend, are the shotgun rider!

Chapter Two
THE CALL

One winter Saturday during my days at Bible college, I sat in my room leisurely making plans with friends for a day of fun when the phone rang. I gave my attention to the interruption and heard a familiar, thickly accented voice. It was Lou, the high school Sunday school teacher from my home church an hour outside the city. Lou Ortez was a man with a great passion for God's work in the lives of young people. He had a friendship with every young person who had come through that church for over thirty years, and he knew where each of them was in their walk with God.

His words were a stark contrast to the plans we were making in the dorm room that morning, and I was certain I must have misunderstood because of his accent. He said he wanted some of the young adult men in the church to begin teaching the high school Sunday school class. He indicated that I was at the top of his list, and he wanted to know when I could begin. His request was delivered like a plan already in motion.

As he unfolded his agenda, I kept trying to back myself out. I felt like I was strapped to the front of a freight train bound for a place I did not want to go. I gave him every reason why he had the wrong guy. I argued that I now lived over an hour away; I said I was barely older than the students in the class; I told him I had no idea what I would teach. For every excuse and argument I offered, he seemed to have already thought through an answer. A few weeks later I found myself in front of thirty high school students stumbling my way through my first teaching experience while Lou

Ortez looked on with great joy and approval.

That was a good chunk of my ministry call right there: no lightning bolts, no voices from the sky, no visiting angels, just a guy on the phone calling up a college kid and asking him to help teach a group of students. Though I struggled through those first experiences, I now know that I was in the process of discovering God's calling on my life.

Many people who enter the ministry struggle with this idea of a calling. They view their entrance to ministry as being like any other decision. They enjoy the work, see it as something they want to do, and sign themselves up. For many, the entrance to ministry just doesn't seem like a call from above. And yet the reality is that if you're serving in the church, and God is using you there, you've entered into a calling. Your ministry is a calling from God. We've gotten away from this important concept in recent years, but perhaps it's time to take another look. After all, it's a biblical concept. Maybe you never saw a lightning bolt or heard the audible voice of God telling you to go into the ministry, but the fact that God does call people into his service is both scriptural and undeniable.

Perhaps this thought makes you feel uncomfortable. Maybe you've witnessed the idea of a calling being misused by someone who may or may not have actually been called. Maybe you know of someone in ministry who uses his or her alleged calling for personal gain or as a club to manipulate people. Or maybe you just don't think your work is big and important enough to constitute a call from God. Perhaps you don't think *you* are important enough. But perhaps a calling isn't as related to a person's following or stature as we might expect. There were plenty of seemingly small folks in Scripture appointed by God for a variety of assignments. Consider Esther, Gideon, or any one of the disciples. All of them were just ordinary folks before they were called into service (and in lots of cases, they still acted like ordinary folks afterward!).

WHO ARE THE CALLED?

From the biblical point of view, all believers are called by God, not just those employed by the church (1 Peter 1:10). For each of us there is the calling to come to Christ and trust him for salvation. Next, there is the calling we experience to live the Christian life, love our enemies, feed the hungry, and care for widows and orphans. Then there is the specific calling that every believer has to complete the good works which God has prepared in advance for him or her to do, as we're told in Ephesians 2:10.

But not everyone will work out that calling in a church or Christian ministry setting. For some, completing their good works happens in part at a secular job. For others, those good works happen predominately through our place of full-time ministry service. For too long the church has gotten away from this idea, considering church work sacred and everything else secular. We've treated those who serve out their sacred calling in the workplace as if their only purpose was to earn money to give to the church where the real ministry happens. This is a mistake, and we must not elevate those who serve in the church above those who don't. Since any calling from God would be sacred, we're all in his sacred work. Those who are called to the church may be the backbone. but we are no more important to her industry than a hand or a foot.

For the sake of this book, however, I want to zero in on those who have received a *call to the church*. There are those who are called predominately to minister outside the church and those who are called to the church. The latter are the senior staff and the shotgun riders, and it's to you I am writing. The church cannot function without some form of organization, and that requires leaders. That being true, there is a call to the church that is unique. In a conversation with Peter, Jesus once said, "And I tell you that you are Peter, and on this rock I will build my church, and the gates of Hades will not overcome it" (Matthew 16:18). God is building his church, and he does that partly through the leaders he puts in place. Sometimes I hear people in the church ranting about the future of the church in such a hopeless, negative way, as if it's going to disintegrate. Have no doubt, Jesus will not let his church die. We don't need to wring our hands in despair. As a matter of fact, he will continue to build his church, just as he's been doing for two thousand years, until he returns. And he will continue to call individuals to take their role in that. God is drawing people to himself, and we get to participate in the venture. That is how he has designed his church to grow.

How Do I Know I'm Called to the Church?

Many people assume that God always calls people by some miraculous sign. My friend Darrin was a youth pastor at a church in the suburbs of Chicago for a number of years. He had a very successful ministry there that had experienced significant growth during his tenure, but he began to wonder if God might be moving him elsewhere. We were all together at a major youth leaders' conference in Atlanta, and Darrin explained the tension he was feeling about what he sensed God might be doing. He didn't want to leave his ministry in Chicago if there was still more that God wanted for him there, but he couldn't deny the tug on his heart for another youth opportunity in Memphis with a ministry called Common Ground.

One afternoon in Atlanta he was really struggling with what to do, and he went out for a walk to talk with God, hoping for some clarity. He was deep in prayer as he walked through midtown Atlanta, losing all sense of direction and time. He now quips that getting lost was just a parody of the bigger turmoil he was experiencing. He was laughing uncomfortably and talking with God about what he felt, asking for direction. Just then he looked up and saw a sign way up high on a building, almost like a message in the clouds. It read "Common Ground." It was so unbelievable that he found his way back to our hotel and explained to his wife, Jane, what had happened to him. He convinced her to go back with him, and together they went looking for that building with the sign. When they finally arrived at the place, the sign was mysteriously gone.

Don't beat yourself up if you didn't see a sign in the clouds when you first felt that you might have a calling. Most of us don't! For those who are tuned in to the heart of the Caller, only simple nudging is required.

So how do you know if you're really called? You might have simply thought ministry sounded like an exciting and rewarding path and it seemed to suit you, and that's all there was to it. Looking back, you probably see some evidence of God's working in leading you in this direction. *And that's all this calling is, really.* It's the fact that God prepared you for what you're doing and led you to a place where your gifts and talents would be used to further his kingdom.

In my own case, I remember a simple yet burning desire to serve God, and I recall going through a period of several years of searching for what that would look like. When I began to serve in the youth ministry at my home church, everything just seemed to come together. It was like a light came on, and I had discovered my fit. This is the simple way God called me to serve in the church, and I am still here twenty years later.

If you happen to be on the other side and trying to figure out whether you're called to the church consider asking yourself the following questions.

Are you gifted for it? Do you have the gifts most prominently used for the ministry you are considering? Most of my energy for almost three decades has been spent in the twin activities of teaching and pastoring.

(More will be said about these gifts, and others, in the next section. But one special note before we move on: While many spiritual gifts can be used outside of the church as well, preaching and teaching are used almost exclusively in the church. So if you have these two gifts, you might want to consider whether God wants you to serve in the church. They don't limit you to being a pastor, or even being a vocational minister, but they may indicate a calling to the church in some capacity.)

Have others encouraged you in this direction? Another great test is the affirmation of others. When you are using your gifts, do others affirm you in them? Do others tell you after you've taught how your teaching has encouraged them? Perhaps you have experienced encouragement from other leaders who have seen you being used by God in an internship or a volunteer role previous to the spot you're in right now. As I look back on that phone call that winter morning, I realize that Lou Ortez saw something I didn't even know was in me. So if other leaders around you are encouraging you to pursue greater involvement in ministry, then it might be worth some consideration and prayer. It just might be that God is using them to give you direction.

Where do you find joy? Do you find joy and fulfillment in serving in your current role as an intern or a volunteer? Is there some particular aspect of ministry that you are drawn to? Could you see yourself doing this full-time? It very well could be that you are built for just such a calling. This is how God often calls people into his service.

How has God led you so far? If you already have some years of ministry under your belt, it might be helpful to jot down a few key events and elements that brought you to your place of ministry service. Occasionally I will review these events in my own life, and I find the reminder greatly encouraging, especially during challenging times. I wouldn't have given that phone call from Lou Ortez another thought except that it came during a period in my life when I felt as though God was speaking to me about the direction of my life. I had been praying for direction, asking him to lead me and show me what it was he wanted me to do. I had to admit that since I'd been praying about it, Lou's phone call just might be part of God's way of directing me. I pray that you too will see that you were and are called to this place of serving him.

The call from Lou, my involvement in an inner-city mission, the sense that God wanted me to serve him—all of these were simply pieces of the puzzle of my calling that God was putting together. No lightning bolt, no voice from heaven, no vision or dream: just some circumstances that came together and pointed me in the direction of the church. That's how the calling of the shotgun rider happens.

The Spirit Gives Gifts

As we've already seen, gifts are one major facet of calling. Maybe you haven't thought about your gifts lately, but they have great implications for you. We know that the Spirit gives gifts and that we received them when we trusted Christ for salvation. These gifts have a purpose in the church according to Ephesians 4:11–12, and that purpose is to equip believers for the works of service that ultimately build up the body of Christ. The point follows that if you've been given these gifts, they are to be used to build his church. You weren't given a gift just so you'd have a memento of receiving Christ. The gifts are meant to be used in the church for the building of the body and the kingdom. So if, for instance, you have the gift of serving, then you are to serve in order to build the kingdom of God.

Likewise, if you've been given the tandem gifts of pastor/teacher, then God must want you to fulfill that role in some way in the building of the church. These two particular gifts come as a package deal, and they work in cooperation to help shepherds fulfill their dual responsibilities of pastoring and teaching. Sometimes you can't really tell the two apart! A friend of mine, an Episcopalian priest, says, "Whenever I'm teaching I'm conscious of the fact that I'm pastoring, and whenever I think I'm pastoring I realize that I'm actually teaching."

God is busy about the building of the church, but he has given his followers the equipment they need to do the work, and some of them he has specifically given the equipment needed to be shepherds. If you have the gifts needed to shepherd, then God must have purposed you and prepared you to do this work for the body of Christ. That purpose and preparation constitute a calling.

It's important to note that there is no age or educational connection to the distribution of the gifts. The pastor/teacher combination is not just given to those who are senior pastors or seminary grads. People who have these gifts are spread throughout the church and represent a variety of ages and positions. By the same token, having the gifts of pastor/teacher doesn't mean that you must be in a paid role. It simply means that you're supposed to use them.

Interestingly, most places in the world have a very different view of vocational ministry than our practice in the West. For example, in India, which along with China has the largest population of Christians, a very small number of pastors are actually paid a full salary. Most who are paid are serving in larger urban churches. The vast majority of pastors who serve in jungle and remote village settings are largely unpaid and often carry the responsibility of several congregations each. I have met many pastors there who serve more than three congregations at once. They remind us of an important truth: When you became a believer you were given spiritual gifts for the purpose of serving God in his church, not primarily so you could receive a paycheck or have a sign on an office door. The question now becomes, how will you use these gifts to serve?

The Characteristics of the Call

The first and key characteristic of a calling to ministry is that every gift is for the purpose of serving in the church. Ministry is all about serving: serving

God, serving his bride, and serving the people outside. A calling to ministry is first and foremost a calling to service for the building of the Lord's church. Sometimes church leaders get this backwards, thinking the church is there to serve their needs. Like a soldier serving his country, we are called to serve God in the church. You never know when you begin serving how that venture will take shape. Where will your service take you? What will be required of you? Will it involve great cost, or perhaps even your life? These are all questions that will only be answered as you obey your call to serve.

One of the dangers of a church calling is that for some, it becomes their sole source of fulfillment. God didn't call you for the purpose of boosting your ego; he called you to serve him because he felt you were fit to meet a need. Your calling is not meant to boost your ego or make you feel good about yourself, so don't expect it to do that for you.

So the object of your calling is to serve and to help people serve in the church. In 1 Thessalonians 2:12–13, Paul says that his ministry was actually the mode God used to accomplish his will in the people's lives. When we serve the Lord using our gifts, it will have God's intended purpose in other's lives.

Another characteristic of the calling to ministry is that it looks to protect. Let me say right from the start that if you are called to ministry in the church, God never meant for you to use your calling as a club or to manipulate your people. Personally, I make it a point to never so much as mention my calling to the people I'm leading. It just comes across like, "Hey, I'm the called one, and you have to do what I say." I also want to avoid giving an impression that I have a calling and those I am serving don't. If God has called you to a task, then do the task and know that he will empower you to do it. You don't need a club, so don't cheapen your calling—all of our callings—by using it to browbeat followers.

By contrast, one of the specific ways church leaders are to use their gifts in service is by guarding the flock. Acts 20:28 says, "Keep watch over yourselves and all the flock of which the Holy Spirit has made you overseers. Be shepherds of the church of God, which He bought with His own blood." This means that we are to protect the unity of the body by not letting criticisms or disagreements be handled incorrectly.

When I was first a youth pastor, an older, more mature mentor challenged me to guard over the things that were said by my students. At the time I didn't realize it, but there wasn't a lot of unity in our group. My friend challenged me not to let any of the students put others down, even in jest. No your-mama's-so-fat jokes, no name-calling, no putting anyone down. At first it seemed a little legalistic, but I soon realized what a change it meant for my group. After we put some standards into place, our group started to grow, and we began to hear comments from visitors who were impacted by the kids in the group. No matter what your particular responsibility is, the importance of making your ministry environment safe cannot be overemphasized. People in your community get beat up by the world all week long. Most have experienced difficult relationships at work or at home, and a congregation that is healthy and caring becomes an oasis for a community. We must serve the flock by guarding over it.

Another characteristic of the calling to ministry is that we are to aim to please God rather than men. Since God is the one who called you, it is to him you're responsible first and foremost. This is one that snags many good shotgun riders. It's so easy to get caught up in trying to please those to whom we report, or those who are our leaders, or perhaps the big givers. Yes, we do certain things because they are required of us, but our focus needs to be on the pleasure of God.

I realize this isn't always an easy focus to maintain. Sometimes our work requirements can become a distraction to our focus. A friend once served at a church where the staff members were required to report their activities hour by hour, giving an accounting of how their time was spent each week. As a salaried staff person with lots of responsibility, she took great offense: it made her feel like she wasn't trusted. Sometimes job requirements become hurdles to pleasing God rather than men, but ultimately Christ is the one who called us, and it's him we are to please. We serve an audience of one.

We face inner battles as well. One of my personal battles happens sometimes when I'm in meetings. The temptation is always there to drop some of my recent accomplishments in conversation or to slip these little nuggets into my prayers. I'm challenged by 1 Thessalonians 2:4, which says that when we speak, we should not try to impress men but to please God. This is so much easier said than done, and for me it can be a real struggle. Every Monday at 3:00 p.m., an alarm goes off in my phone's calendar as an intentional interruption just about the time we are beginning to enter the business portion of our weekly staff meeting. The calendar item says, "YOUR GOD IS NOT IN THIS ROOM!" I need this reminder that my true God is not the people I work with or the person I report to, and I pause each time it goes off and have a short conversation with God—the real God, who thankfully is with me everywhere!—about my struggle.

There is a very real temptation even for good shotgun riders to try to impress others with the things we've done in ministry, especially those up the food chain. This is really counterproductive to how God wants to work through us. Remember that God wants to use us in our weakness, and it's through that very weakness that he is often most glorified.

Another aspect of our calling is that when we speak, we should speak as though speaking for God. This means that we should be very careful of what we say whenever we speak. I try to remember to whisper a prayer, asking God to give wisdom, when I'm asked to speak. Early on, one of my ministry mentors challenged me to pray before I pick up the phone or begin a conversation. I want to say what God would have me say, and I need his help because my own inclination is to go about vomiting out the first thing that pops into my head. When we speak, we should be most concerned about God's agenda, not our own.

There tend to be two extremes in the church. At each end of the spectrum are dangers to be avoided. On the one hand, there are those who hold that they regularly speak the words of God. The danger for these folks may be the assumption that just because their mouth is moving, God is speaking. At the other extreme there are those who would say that God's messages are never delivered through humans today. My point is not to debate the validity of charismatic gifts, but rather to highlight the need to give respect to the position you are in. Whether or not you believe that your words contain an actual message from God to your people, your words will either cause them to walk closer with God or potentially drive them away. Before you answer that phone call, before you begin that conversation, before you open your mouth, take a moment to ask God to make your words matter. Ask him to help you convey the truths of his Word to people. Show that you understand how vital your shepherding role is and how deeply you depend on him.

The Implications of Your Calling

If God does call people into the ministry, there must be some importance attached to what he has asked them to do. In this section, I want to explore just a few of the implications of a calling.

First, if we are called by God to a task or responsibility, then it would seem fitting to treat that responsibility with the importance of a God-sized call. I love the story of Moses standing before the burning bush. Here's Moses trembling in front of the bush, speaking with God, and what's the first thing God says? "Take off your shoes, for you're standing on holy ground." We have to ask, why was the ground on which Moses was standing holy? It was holy for several reasons.

First, it was holy because God was there. Any place where God is standing is going to be a holy place. The presence of God recharacterizes the very ground on which we stand. God's presence always does that. When God moves in and shows up, make sure to take note. Pause in reverent worship, for you have a momentary view into the activity of a holy and powerful God.

The ground was also holy because God was announcing a new direction for his people. God told Moses that when he had brought the people out of Egypt, they would worship God on that very mountain—and they did (Exodus 19:2). Sometimes when God met people in their need, they were told to set up a monument as a reminder of what he did, like when the Israelites crossed the Jordan in Joshua 3 and 4. There the people were told to set up stones at the place where they had crossed the Jordan. When God brings about a new plan, we should mark that place, noting that things were one way before that time and a different way afterward, and we should see that as an opportunity to pause in reverent worship.

After I got out of college, I worked at my home church for a final and third summer as an intern. That internship turned into a yearlong experience while I prayed about what God would have for me next. I fully expected that he had a long-term plan for me at that church, but toward the end of that year it became crystal clear that God was moving me to another church in a different state. After I had come to terms with this, I remember spending most of an afternoon in the balcony of the church praying and thanking God for the three summers and one year there serving him and learning about ministry. As I prayed, I wept through much of the afternoon, knowing that this was a marker in God's work in my life and calling. For me, that balcony was my own holy ground. Since that time, there have been several other holy grounds where God has moved in my life and ministry. It's good to have markers to remind us of God's work in our lives.

Finally, the ground was holy because Moses was receiving a holy assignment. How do I know it was a holy assignment? It was a holy assignment because it came from a holy God. Anything a holy God asks you to do is a holy assignment and comes with an amount of his authority and blessing.

After I was out of college I worked part time in a lumberyard. I spent much of my time making deliveries, and I loved the work. David, the boss, would load the truck and strap down the cargo. After this was finished, he would take me aside for "the talk," which always followed the same pattern. First, he gave the details of the delivery: the location, the contact person, etc. Then together, we would walk through a safety check of the load, checking the straps and position of each item. I was never sure if this was for his peace of mind or for my training or both. Then he would give strict instructions regarding the speed limit on various roads along the route and how to safely drop the load or back it into a loading dock.

While he was giving his talk, he always held the keys between his forefinger and thumb with his arm outstretched as if to make a point about the transfer of responsibility. Then finally there was the handoff: the moment when the keys were placed in my hand. A call to serve in the church is much like that. There is the readying for the ride, and then there is the moment when the keys are handed over.

At this point, it's incredibly important to remember that this is a holy assignment. You're in this ministry position in which God has placed you. Your calling has been confirmed by other leaders and by the response of people to whom you have ministered. You have found great pleasure in the use of your spiritual gifts in the church. God has placed you here, and the only difference between your calling and the calling of Moses is that you didn't have God speak to you from a burning bush. Maybe your entrance to your assignment wasn't as obvious as Moses's call, but make no mistake, you are in the place to which God has led you.

When you see your assignment in this way, it will cause you to view it in a new light. You are where God is at work in the lives of people, and he has chosen to use you as his emissary. You have a holy assignment and have been handed the keys to an important task, and you must treat it with great reverence. Sometimes we get frustrated with the people God has called us to work with, and it's good to remind ourselves that we are to be God's tools in their lives. I must confess that this thought has often kept me from going off on one of the sheep. Sometimes we just need to be reminded that it's God's work; God's calling.

A second implication of calling is that God's calling comes with a certain amount of his authority. I once was having a difficult time following through with some changes that I knew would upset a couple of people on my staff. I knew this because they had already spoken against me on the issue. These were changes that several others on the staff and I had prayed about and had become convinced God wanted us to make. I mentioned this to Randy, my senior pastor, and he said something to me that was a great encouragement. He said, "Doug, you need to stand on your pastoral authority and do what you feel God wants you to do." How many times in ministry I have cowered because I didn't want to go head-to-head with someone over some plan or because I just didn't have the energy to put up a fight! If God has called us to a ministry, then we have his authority to act within it.

There is the temptation to be constantly checking our popularity rating to see if we have enough chips stored up to move forward with a particular decision. This is wrong-headed because it's the shepherd who is supposed to lead the sheep, not the other way around. We get our direction from God, not through ministry chips that we've managed to store up. Leaders are supposed to lead. This doesn't give us the excuse to ramrod agendas or be heavy-handed with people, but it does mean that we should move forward with confidence when we believe God wants us to do so.

At the same time, authority can be misused. David used his position to sleep with Bathsheba, Samson gave away the secret to his power, Moses killed an Egyptian, and Abraham lied about his wife. What makes us think that we would be any less likely candidates to misuse our position or authority? God's authority is not to be used at will, at least not at *our* will, because it is his will to which that authority is attached. For that reason, the more authority we have, the more important it is that we walk with humility before God and man.

A third implication is that we should handle our ministry career with great care. I would say the same thing about any calling, but my concern here is for my friends who are living out a call to the church. Since God is the One who calls his people into his service, those places of service deserve a special kind of reverence. Make ministry moves only after spending lots of time in prayer and gaining wisdom from other Christian leaders. I know that there has been a shift over the years in the way that church leaders move from one position to another, but there is something really God-honoring about taking significant time to prayerfully consider a ministry move. Your calling is wrought out through a conversation between you and God. Yes, taking note of your abilities and how God has wired you is helpful; yes, considering the advice of other ministry mentors is useful. For sure, the response of those we lead and minister to is helpful in determining God's leading. But ultimately, it comes down to an ongoing conversation with our Lord. This is the cement of our calling. He is the one who gifts you and calls you. He is the One who has ordained the direction of your steps.

Sometimes well-meaning or not so well-meaning Christians will bring into question your calling. Once, just before I was about to begin a teaching time, one of the girls in the youth group came up to me and asked, "How is there any way you can say you belong in the ministry? You're not called to ministry." Her words stung, but I came to realize that she was way out of line. Only God holds authority over our calling.

The holiness of a calling to ministry has repercussions for the handling of church leaders as well. We should encourage our church leadership to handle personnel issues with care. At times leaders shift the workloads of their staff around without giving consideration to the particular giftedness and calling of the individuals concerned. Staff changes are made like every-day business transactions with little thought or care for the individuals, their callings, or even their families.

Too often we borrow misapplied strategies from the business world for help in managing affairs. Some great principles can be learned from the business world, but the church is not a business. Often, the main point of business methods is to cut costs. A friend of mine serves in a church that runs itself in this way. The conversation in board meetings is always about how to cut costs and be more efficient. Rather than asking how the church can use its available funds for the kingdom, the leaders' focus is how to do ministry for less money, choking out vitality and growth. Their motivation is always to save more and spend less. Sadly, that church is dying today. The people who attend your church are sheep, not shareholders; they are called to be servants, not act as owners. The same is true for us. The people who lead them are not directors but spiritual leaders who are to equip them for works of service.

QUALIFIED?

I receive a regular phone call from a headhunter company that looks to fill certain ministry positions around the country, often high-profile positions. The phone conversation usually begins like this: "Doug, I've called because your name has come up in conversation here in our office, and we wanted to present a ministry opportunity that we feel would be a strategic move for you." Then the young man on the other end of the phone will begin to tell me what a great ministry opportunity this particular church would be.

Almost always, the available position is one that is less suited to my giftedness and experience, and it's usually one for which I'm overqualified. These people are acting as agents seeking to fill a spot with the most qualified person they can find. Nothing wrong with that, right? Unless of course the person you're trying to lure has been called by God to something else or somewhere else.

I used to get flattered to think that my name came up in some office somewhere, that someone wanted me to consider coming to interview for a position (along with the fifty other pastors they called, of course). I've since learned that this company keeps files of pastors, and every time a new person comes to work at their company, that person goes through the files and tries to find someone to fill an opening so he or she can receive a commission. Perhaps you too, feel uncomfortable with the brokering of a sacred call.

If you feel strongly that you are called to ministry, you may wonder whether you are qualified. So often ministry job descriptions are written in such a way that you wonder if even the apostle Paul would qualify. What about the fact that God chooses the weak things of this world to confound the wise? Didn't just about every servant of God in the Bible have some sort of defect? Moses had a speech impediment, Jonah was prejudiced, and David was just a boy when he slew Goliath. The list goes on. All of these men would get overlooked by ministry headhunters, and maybe you would too. But that's okay—if God has called you, he will also gift and qualify you. Don't sell your calling short. You are the shotgun rider.

THE CALL CODE

1. *Never use your call as a tool to manipulate others.*

   If you're really called then the bending of hearts won't happen through manipulation but rather through the work of the Holy Spirit.

   Anything less shows you really don't trust the One who called you.

2. *Never allow the comments of others regarding your calling to dwell in your thinking.*

   This means negative comments as well as positive ones.

   The essence of your calling is seated in a conversation with God, not with mortals.

3. *Make all life decisions after weeks and months of conversation with the One who called you.*

   Career moves require the direction and blessing of your God. Don't always expect a career move to make sense, humanly speaking.

   Getting married, having children, and adopting children are all invitations for others to join you in your adventure with God.

4. *Never allow others to poke fun at what you do.*

   "You only work Sundays and Wednesdays."

   "Since we have a hired holy man here, he can ask the blessing over the meal."

5. *Don't waste your time talking about your calling with your disciples.*

   It may only be perceived as prideful.

   What will be accomplished by telling others you're called?

   Let them see the evidence of your calling in your life and in your walk with God.

CHAPTER THREE

THE MANDATE

In one of the cities where I lived, a church was advertising on a billboard that read "Experience More." I recently saw another church billboard that read "Not your mother's church." I'm all for creative marketing, but if the goal of our church is simply to produce a better product than other churches, we've missed the purpose and design of the church. We find the church's purpose in Matthew 28:19–20. We are called to be salt and light to a dark world, not just provide a better option than the church your mom went to.

When I was sixteen, I got my first official job as a clerk in a department store. When I was offered the position, they gave me a document entitled "Job Description." On this document were listed all of the responsibilities I had to complete. It gave me a good idea of what I would be doing each day on the job. In the church where I serve, we have developed job descriptions for all of the paid workers and for many of the volunteer positions as well. This helps the Sunday school teacher, the worship leader, and the greeter know what we would like them to do.

We must ask ourselves, "What is the job description for the shotgun rider? Where in the Bible do we find such a description?" The answer is found in the commission that Jesus gave to his followers:

Therefore go and make disciples of all nations, baptizing them in the name of the Father and of the Son, and of the Holy Spirit, and teaching them to obey everything I have commanded you. And surely I am with you always, to the very end of the age.

MATTHEW 28:19–20

Why is this our mandate? Of all the Scriptures we could use as our main objective for our ministry and calling, why is this the one?

To start with, the Great Commission is the mandate for the church as a whole. This is the church's main job description, and so it belongs to every ministry leader in the church. Matthew 28:19–20 is our ultimate assignment regardless of our title. Our job is to make disciples. Now we must ask, "What is the process of doing that?" The passage tells us that we are to accomplish the task of disciple-making by teaching. By teaching what? By teaching them to obey everything Christ has commanded us. Teaching is the mode of communicating the gospel, and it should aim at helping students be obedient disciples. And it happens in many ways—not just through sermons or Bible studies or Sunday school lectures. "My ministry is about worship," you say, but I say that in some way your ministry of worship serves the greater purpose of the Great Commission. Or perhaps you're the small group pastor and you say, "Wait, I'm about building small groups where intimate fellowship and growth happens." Ultimately, your ministry too fulfills the Great Commission. All ministries in the church work together to help fulfill the job description of the church. Mathew 28:19–20 tells us that the main job of every believer is ultimately to make disciples. In fact, the only imperative in the passage is to make disciples. Going, baptizing, and teaching are all actually dependent clauses in the passage. That means teaching serves the purpose of making disciples. So if we happen to be teaching and we are going to give our students biblical content, then we will do it to help them be disciples of Christ. If we are doing activities with our team, then those activities should, in some way, help them follow Christ. If we are going to do evangelism, it is because evangelism is the first step in making a disciple.

OWNING THE GOAL

When I first considered the possibility of becoming a youth pastor, I had already begun to cut my teeth in an internship at my home church. Someone suggested that I attend a ministry seminar. At the time I questioned the suggestion, wondering what more I could need than what I had received in my Bible college training. (Admittedly, many of us thought we were God's gift to the church when we were fresh out of Bible college or seminary!) But someone else had offered to pay my way, and so I went. I would later go on to attend more of these seminars and even become a trainer with that organization. Looking back, I credit that training as giving me the purpose I needed to remain focused on the right priorities in ministry.

It was through that experience that I began to own the Great Commission as my overriding goal for what I knew I needed to be about in ministry. Sure, I'd heard the Great Commission preached about at our church's mission conferences and occasionally in sermons, but I'd never really owned it as my own passion and priority until my involvement with this organization.

I question whether I'd still be in ministry today if it wasn't for what I gained through that experience. If it's your plan to remain in ministry long-term, having a support system is absolutely necessary. You can find one through your denomination or through a training organization, but you must find it if you want to survive. In one of the locations where I served, finding camaraderie, fellowship, and support was somewhat challenging, so I got together with some local ministry peers and we created a group ourselves. That ministry alliance of youth leaders is still functioning today.

Maintaining Your Focus

Sometimes our ministry vision gets out of focus. One day as I was driving down the highway in my car, I noticed something peculiar: there was a slight fuzziness to the words on each sign. I reached for something to wipe the window, thinking there was a smudge on the windshield, but the blurriness was still there. I surmised there must be something on the outside, so I flipped on the windshield wipers, and still the blurriness remained. In an effort to discover the source of the blur I experimented by first closing my left eye and then closing my right, reading the words with each eye in turn. To my surprise, I learned that my right eye was having trouble seeing clearly. My eyesight was showing its age! Not long after that I found myself wearing glasses, and I could again see what was once out of focus and blurry.

Even good ministry leaders find their perspective out of focus at times. For instance, we might focus on the teaching of content only, becoming so set on getting the facts of the Bible to our people that we forget what purpose those facts are supposed to serve. The content of the Bible is important, but no matter what our role is, we need to focus on more than just dumping information.

Some youth leaders are tempted to make their ministry only about having fun. They see their most important role as keeping the youth ministry fun and exciting. I knew a youth pastor who succumbed to this focus. Every event he planned had to be bigger and better than the previous one, and they became so expensive and outlandish that he simply couldn't keep up. The students demanded that he keep producing events that were better each time. Eventually he burned out and left the ministry. Having fun while learning is not in itself a bad thing—in fact, we could argue that making learning fun might actually make our teaching more effective. However, when this becomes your main purpose, students may lose interest if the excitement level ever drops because they too have begun to think that the main purpose of the youth group is to have fun.

Another false focus is thinking only of the outward appearance of those we lead. The leader or teacher who makes this mistake sees only what is outwardly visible in those he is responsible for. This teacher has forgotten that the Bible says man sees the outward appearance but God sees the heart (1 Samuel 16:7). These folks teach their students that what one says or does determines whether one is a Christian. Certainly we must teach about things that are visible on the outside; as Scripture says, "Even small children are known by their actions" (Proverbs 20:11). But a higher priority is that we are developing hearts that are like Christ's, and that is a much bigger challenge.

Yet another fuzzy perspective is focusing on evangelism only. Certainly evangelism is important. Accepting Christ is indeed the first and most important step in the Christian life. But if we make evangelism our only focus, we will never see our followers grow beyond baby Christians. The Bible teaches that disciples should grow and learn to feed on solid food, not only on milk (1 Corinthians 3:2).

It's easy, over time, to lose the primary focus of our calling, and many have never understood the main purpose for their assignment in the first place. Thankfully, our primary focus isn't a secret, and it isn't hard to understand. The main purpose of the shotgun rider must be to make disciples in everything we do.

You Have His Authority

The encouraging factor is that we do this in the authority of Jesus Christ. This is clear in the wording of the Great Commission itself! He has granted us the power to make disciples and to do it well. We are also reminded that he is with us in this assignment to the very end. When we are about the business of the Great Commission, we go in the name of Jesus, and he desires for us to be successful. He will make sure the job is accomplished. This doesn't mean that every assignment will go perfectly or that every shotgun rider will always have great success in everything. It doesn't mean that every one of our followers will turn into a great disciple. It just means that God wants us to be effective leaders, and he will enable us to do what he's called us to do.

Knowing that the Holy Spirit is working and that we are laboring under the authority of Christ, we can approach the task with confidence. While we are about the business of the Great Commission, we can press on with great confidence because God is in it. Success in ministry does not depend only on human effort but on God's power and authority. Sometimes we are tempted to have a casual attitude about our ministry, wondering if we are doing any good as we lead. We should confess our lack of confidence and trust in God, because he is the one who gives us the authority and power for leading, and we can trust that he wants us to be successful in the mandate given to us.

CHAPTER FOUR

WHO'S UNDER YOUR TIN ROOF?

I didn't learn it in seminary, and I didn't get it at a pastor's conference. The most important ministry lesson I ever learned I got sitting under a tin roof in the salty Caribbean air.

Pretty quickly when you arrive at your first ministry post, you realize there are things you weren't taught in seminary or Bible college. As it turns out, in fact, *most* of the things we need in ministry are picked up along the way from friends or mentors or plain old experience. Sometimes you acquire them by trial and error. Ministry itself is a great teacher and a whole lot cheaper than seminary or Bible college.

Most seminary graduates admit having little to no training in the most important roles and functions we fulfill. How to shepherd our people is one such gap. It's what most of our energy is spent on, yet it's a task for which most of us received little formal training. Shepherding is a key part of making disciples and fulfilling our mandate. People skills are essential for the job: how to do conflict resolution well, how to deal with leaders who cause dissension. And why is it that I was never taught in seminary how to handle a complaint against me? My own total formal training in conflict resolution came in the form of one two-hour breakout seminar at a pastor's conference, which was too little and too late for the situations I was involved in at the time. And those are just the areas where we need to take care of ourselves and our peers—learning to care properly for those who are under our leadership is a whole other ball game.

My tin roof experience happened near the end of a ten-day mission trip to the Dominican Republic. It had been a great week, complete with everything a good mission trip should have: a robust case of Montezuma's, numerous opportunities to embarrass my hosts by butchering their language, and to top it all off, a scuffle with a truckload of military police who accosted one of the street kids near the church intending to beat the coconut juice out of him. It had been memorable and gave me plenty of new reasons to pray for our missionary friends...but there was more.

That afternoon we had been working on our concrete project with plenty of locals at our side. Everyone knows that all good mission trips involve some kind of concrete work, and every time we showed up at the church, young men appeared out of nowhere to assist us with ours. One by one they would slip through the gate, and before we knew it, there would be several dozen young men working alongside us. I kept wondering where they came from and how they knew we were there, and then I noticed something interesting. Most of them seemed to have a deep connection to our missionary host, Joaquin. He was a thoughtful and caring leader, and you could tell that his love for these young men ran deep.

As the afternoon wore on, gray clouds began to build overhead, fueling a growing frenzy among our companions. They seemed to know what was coming. Then, with one sharp crack, the sky opened up and let loose a downpour so thick you could sense the added weight of the rain on your clothes before you ever felt the wetness hit your skin.

People scattered in all directions in an effort to find cover, and when the initial excitement died down, I found myself standing under the tin roof of the church's only meeting space. I hadn't paid much attention to the fact that the roof was tin until I heard the deafening roar above us. It was so loud that any conversation required shouts. Looking out through the barred windows, I saw palm trees swaying in time with sheets of soaking rain. I chuckled uncomfortably as I watched the rest of my group pile into the van and drive away, leaving me behind. As the rain slowed to a drizzle, the stage was set for a God moment that would leave me a different person.

Joaquin motioned for the young men to circle up chairs for some kind of meeting, and without hesitation he insisted that I join in. As the rain rumbled on overhead, there was a momentary pause in the room as if something was about to happen. It was clear that the Holy Spirit was about to go to work. To this day I cannot explain it—there was nothing in my straight-up Baptist/Bible Church preparedness training for what happened in that mist-filled air below the tin roof. God met me there that afternoon, and I left a different person than when I came in.

There I was, the lone pasty foreigner, pale and out of place on so many levels. I was, in that moment, a spiritual gringo about to get schooled in the classroom of ministry life. I know now that God designed that circle to hand off some tools I'd need along the way, some vital bits he knew could never be acquired in a seminary classroom. That afternoon was a turning point in my ministry journey, and I knew I could not go back and continue on in the same way.

Joaquin began with a few initial remarks as I strained to pick out familiar Spanish words in an effort to get some feel for what was happening. I could tell this was important only by the tone in his voice. After he finished his initial remarks, he turned to the young man next to him and began to address him in encouraging tones. The young man seemed to hang on his every word in appreciation.

As Joaquin made his way around the circle, speaking to each protégé, energy and passion poured straight from his soul. Some things you get without the necessity of words, and his deep love for these guys was like that. It was obvious he wanted God's best for each of them. It brought me to tears even though I knew little of what was actually said. I tried to swallow back the painful lump swelling in the bottom of my throat. His tone of urgency seemed to build as he worked his way around the circle toward me.

When we first sat down, Ronaldo had plopped into the seat next to me. I'd grown fond of him that week, and he seemed to take a specific interest in instructing me on the proper way to hold a hammer or the best way to cut a piece of rebar. Though I couldn't speak much with him, I felt a connection, and I looked for him every day at the project. Joaquin began to speak to Ronaldo as giant tears now rolled freely down his cheeks. Whatever this was about, Ronaldo was uncomfortable talking about it, and he shifted in the metal chair. Joaquin's most passionate words, it seemed, had been saved for my new friend. Then Joaquin began to translate for me what he had been saying.

He said, "Felix here," pointing to the young man seated next to him, "began his walk with Jesus about a year ago but has stopped growing and we've been talking about how to get back on a growing path. Jose," pointing to the next guy, "is growing and is the only Christian in his family, and I shared with him some of the ways that I've been praying for him. Juan is next, and he has some trouble at home. You see, his father is abusive to his mother and younger brothers, and he's really torn up about it. Last Sunday he brought his father to church, and he hopes he'll come to know Jesus."

It seemed that each story became more and more serious, and I wondered if they'd been intentionally placed in this order. Then he came to Ronaldo, who by this time was sitting stiffly in his chair. "Ronaldo needs to end his relationship with his girlfriend and return to his wife. His children are really upset, and he's left them with no sort of income."

By the time he finished with my young friend, I was choking back sobs. Joaquin continued on around the room, but I didn't hear much after that. I was still stuck on "return to his wife." All that week Ronaldo had worked alongside of us, and I never imagined that he was in such turmoil. I was awakened to the needs under the tin roof that rainy afternoon. Even though I couldn't speak much of the language, I had become part of the circle and the circle had become part of me. More than anything, I was moved by the love and care of my friend for his followers. I knew I had to do ministry differently when I went home. It was time to begin circling up the people under my own tin roof and loving them the way Joaquin loved his guys.

It's a fact we become aware of soon after we begin in ministry: it's simply too easy to get all caught up in ministry with things that don't really matter. We create events and programs that take on a life of their own, and we find ourselves with the proverbial ball and chain buckled around our ankle, or worse, our neck. Programs, though they may have begun with the greatest of motivations, determine our schedules and demand our time and attention. Some even seem to have lost their original purpose, and we wonder why we continue to pump our time and resources into them.

So here I was, barely a year into my first ministry experience and rechecking my programs and involvements. It was as if the whole grid had changed. I wanted to rethink everything in light of my newfound desire to see lives changed and make an eternal impact. The drive to busy myself with programs and events, even fun or exciting ones, now seemed meaningless if somehow they didn't touch on God's work in people's lives. I wanted to see lives changed up close.

I had to ask myself, "Into whose life am I speaking truth? Whose prayer burdens am I helping to carry? Who is it who's sitting under my tin roof?" I ask you the same question: Who is it who's sitting under your roof? Perhaps they're serving each week in your ministry. Maybe they're in your youth group or on your worship team. Maybe they show up at small group every week. Don't ever think that one of them is there by mistake or that somehow their presence is unrelated to your calling to shepherd and develop disciples of Jesus. Not one of them is there by happenstance or by accident.

I've had occasional opportunities through the years to travel back to that same church. Things have changed over time. The tin roof is gone now—it's been replaced by concrete—and that space below is now used for storage. Most of those young men, now grown, are gone too, scattered to various other places. Some of them, like Ronaldo, are pastors. Some are missionaries. The imprint of the shepherd lives on in every one of them. Sometimes when I'm there, I ask the caretaker to open the old room so I can go in and have a few moments to myself to sit and reflect. I always thank God for that afternoon when he met me under the tin roof and showed me what it means to be a shepherd. I've never been the same person since, and I only hope I can be half the shepherd my friend Joaquin is.

So when was the last time you sat and just listened to someone in your circle? When was the last time you told them how you're praying for them? How well do you know what's really going on at home? Can you name the spiritual challenges each one in your circle faces? Can you even name the faces in your circle?

One of the things I've learned about personal pain and spiritual growth is that they often show up together. The times in my own life when I learned to trust God more, love more, or depend more on him were lessons generally learned in pain. I suspect the same is true for you, and I imagine the same is true for the people we serve and work alongside in ministry. If we're going to be connected with them at the crossroads where God will meet them, we're going to want to be connected with them in meaningful ways.

It's time to enter the circle and care for people beyond whatever volunteer service they bring to your ministry or how they fill up the room at events or meetings. They are people: persons has God placed in your care, not just slots that got filled by Jim or Katie or that tall guy with the bushy hair. They have names and they have families and friends, and they are your sheep. The thing about sheep is they all have stories and they all need a shepherd. They want a shepherd, yes, every one of them. So I ask you again, who is under your tin roof?

LEAD THEM

If there's one thing that people need and want, it's to be led. I find that the best way to start leading them is by being involved in their lives. Lead them by knowing the names of their kids and what they struggle with. Don't lead them by being prescriptive: be a leader by listening. Howard Hendricks used to repeat a quote attributed to Theodore Roosevelt: "People won't care how much you know until they know how much you care." Be the leader who cares, and they will be motivated to follow you.

Being a listening leader means you must also be available and approachable. Don't lead from an ivory tower; lead from the ground. Know that this means you will have to structure your schedule so you are available. You can't be so busy that your people feel like they're keeping you from your real work. Too many leaders are so busy that they don't have the time for the real ministry of being a shepherd. Let them know by your actions that caring for them is your main concern.

Leading your leaders and others has to happen up close. This means you need to be where they are. Never make excuses for this. In one of my youth ministries, the youth leaders and I and even some of the student leaders were in the habit of staying out late together after our Wednesday night youth meetings. We'd end up at one of the leader's homes for a late-night ping-pong tournament, or we'd find a restaurant and stay until it closed.

Sometimes we'd go to a late-night movie. The gatherings rarely broke up before 1:00 a.m. These were important times of relationship building and growth. Some of our greatest times of spiritual connectedness happened over ping-pong or chips and queso. When Thursday morning came, each of us would be dragging ourselves into our workplaces or our schools. But it was absolutely worth it. Early on I set the record straight around the church office that this was not just a party after the youth meeting, this was ministry, this was iron sharpening iron, and yes, it was fun too. I have to believe that God looked down and was pleased because we were often talking about him and his work in our lives.

As you spend time with your volunteer leaders, remember to show them the big picture. Every volunteer wants to see and understand how their particular place of service fits in. Be a leader by helping them feel a part of what's going on. Help them see why what they do is important. There is a sixty-something couple that volunteers in our Sunday school. Each week they help keep the attendance records. They sit in an office removed from most of the classes. They rarely actually go into a room, and they seldom have conversations with the teachers. Occasionally I will remind them why what they do is important. I want them to feel a part of what's going on. I want them to know what they do matters in the big scheme.

LOVE THEM

Lead your leaders, and those you are serving, by loving them. Sometimes we become wrongly focused on trying to manufacture growth in our ministries and the church. All real ministry growth flows from love. I'm not saying that *church growth* flows from love, but that growth in people's lives does. You can grow a big church and not have an ounce of love in sight. (And you can have a big church without real disciples.) Or you can make it your goal to love people as Jesus did, and you will likely still experience growth. Those things that only Christ can accomplish will and must be birthed out of your love.

For the nearly two decades I spent as a youth pastor, I began every school year with four to six weeks emphasizing love. Why? Because I knew that all spiritual growth involves love. We taught on love, and we challenged the students to love their enemies. We had activities to get love flowing. Each week I challenged them to love others in specific ways, through writing a note or some gesture of kindness. On occasion I would hand out notecards and tell my students we were going to write love cards for the next thirty minutes. I would challenge them to express love to others around them in writing and deliver the note before going on to the next one. I told them that the note could be a compliment or something that they appreciate about the other. I would ask them to begin with someone they hadn't spoken to in a while; that way they wouldn't just write notes to their friends. Sometimes it was a challenge to get them to join me in the exercise, but once we finished, the students almost always asked me to do it again soon. The outflow of these activities was amazing, and the changed atmosphere in our group would be evident each year.

Jesus once said, "By this everyone will know you are my disciples, if you love one another" (John 13:35). Others will know we are Christians by our love. Not by our cool T-shirt or the background on our homepage or the bumper sticker on our car. No, they will know we are Christians by our love. I encourage you especially to develop this focus among your leadership team. There is no place more important for this love to begin than among your leaders. If your key leaders don't get it, how will the message ever make it to the youth group or the choir or your small group?

Build Them

Finally, lead others by building into them. Equip them for works of service. Teach them everything you needed to learn to get to where you are, not in a professional sense but in a spiritual one. Teach them how to do what you've given them to do, and don't do this in a bomb drop but over long periods of time and in bite-size, understandable chunks as you live life with them.

Lead them by building them up. Always lead from the positive. I know a leader who leads from the negative, always telling his volunteers what they are doing wrong. His ministry has become a revolving door because people tire of the constant barrage of negativity.

Lead them by appreciating not just what they do for you but how they're equipped to do it. Recognize that God has given them gifts to serve.

Show them that you appreciate that they are using their gifts to serve in your area.

Lead them also by challenging them to grow. Like my friend Joaquin, involvement in the personal side of others' lives is necessary if we are to shepherd them. If we see them solely as a means to an end, like a way to get a program staffed or an event filled, then it's not necessary to get too personal with them, is it? If however we intend to truly lead and shepherd them, then getting into their lives is a must. Spiritual growth is intimately married to relationship. It was that way even with Jesus' followers. He didn't just give his disciples a bunch of work to do, he built relationships with them and taught them along the way as a part of his interaction with them. Treat others like Jesus treated his disciples, and you will have an influence in their lives.

Don't be afraid to be a shepherd. Look at it as the main thing rather than a side thing. See it as your privilege to shepherd others, because you, my friend, are the shotgun rider.

CHAPTER FIVE

RIDING WITH OTHERS

When I was in high school I had a friend named Ron who bought a 1977 Chevy Malibu Classic. It had a 305 V8 and the most amazing paint job. At the time that car was already a few years old but on its way to being considered a classic, and his was in pristine condition. There were only a few hundred of these cars made, so it was a real find. I will never forget the way heads would turn when we were out riding around. The car was his baby and so, not surprisingly, he took amazing care of it.

I remember the day Ron first asked me if I wanted to go for a ride. He was going to drive two hours up to Wisconsin to visit some mutual friends. Before I got in the car, he stopped me and told me that he had a few instructions if I was going to ride along. I was not to place my arm out the window because over time the oil from skin would deteriorate the paint. I was not to put my feet on anything but the floor, and I was not to eat or drink anything in the car. I remember joking that I felt like I was having a job interview. He didn't laugh.

I can't help but make the connection to ministry life. As long as you are the shotgun rider, you will have challenges to face as you ride along with others. There will be ample expectations both spoken and unspoken, and plenty of opportunities to mess up.

PLAYING TEAM BALL

My favorite sport has always been basketball. I love the athleticism involved and the fast pace of the game. When I was a youth minister, I tried to go to every home game at the local high school so I could be where my students were, and then later, when my oldest son began to play, I found myself again logging in courtside hours. There were tournaments and summer clinics and spring and fall leagues and the school team as well. Now that our fine city has an NBA team, I find myself once again enthralled with the game.

One of the things I love about basketball is that to be played well, it has to be played as a team. It's a natural law of the game. Whether you're talking about a pickup game at the park or the NBA, no team does well that doesn't play team ball.

When you watch the game you realize that not everyone understands this. Basketball seems to attract hotshots—those players who want to show off their moves and their dunking ability. But just because a team has a couple of hotshots doesn't mean they can win on the court. Nothing gets me more excited than to see a team of average skilled players go up against a team of showoffs and win simply because they knew how to play as a team and the more highly skilled opponents didn't.

It's the same on a church staff. The best staff environments, the most motivating teams, are the ones that play well together. On the other hand, nothing is more frustrating than being part of a staff or volunteer team where some hotshot, or several, don't play team ball but rather hog the ball and play for themselves.

A senior pastor who was a family friend once pursued me to join his church staff. (I've since learned that there are right and wrong ways to go about making a ministry career move, and this is not a route I would recommend.) The church leadership had several hiring goals, and they made it clear they were looking to bring on the best they could afford so they could have the best possible team. Several staff members were hired just after I was, and soon the leadership of the church was calling us the Dream Team. I have to admit I was a little flattered at the time, yet something about it didn't sit right with me. I quickly realized that we couldn't succeed if we didn't play like a team. Just like in basketball, a staff of hotshots might look impressive at first but will accomplish less together, and getting anywhere will require longer and take more effort.

As shotgun riders, we're often in positions of leadership. So how do we take the principle of team ball and apply it to our own staff situation? How do we encourage team play on our staff? For starters, know that you can't control what others do, but you can start with yourself and build from there.

As a leader you will do well to play team ball with anyone who will join you, even if it's not a part of the culture of your staff overall. A team where two or three people are playing team ball is better any day than a team where no one does, and if a few are playing like a team, others will take note and perhaps join in. (We'll look more at working with a difficult situation that's out of your control in the next chapter.)

Teamwork has to start somewhere. When you form your team, make sure to declare among yourselves what your common goals and values are. Then do your best to foster an environment where everyone plays team ball.

BUILDING TRUST

In order for there to be a true team atmosphere, there has to be trust among team members. Trust is imperative because in ministry, you have to know that the team members will stick up for each other and protect one another. If team cohesion begins to crumble, it eats away at the whole team's ability to move forward.

Team members must trust each other. Be sure that whatever qualities you instill in your team will filter on down through the ranks. When I first came to one of the churches where I served, there were deep roots of suspicion and mistrust among some key ministry leaders. There were turf wars everywhere I turned. There were labels on cabinets that read, "Mrs. Johnson's class. KEEP OUT!" After getting to know Mrs. Johnson, I realized there was little for her to worry about. Her wombat-like personality was reason enough to steer clear of both her and her cabinet! Certain ministries were required to pay for supplies used from the supply room—for no reason other than those who stocked the supply room wanted it that way. Numerous times I was called in to an "emergency meeting" because someone's scissors had disappeared or because a poster had inadvertently been hung on another ministry's wall space.

As I dug into the church background a little more, what I discovered was that this culture of mistrust and suspicion had been fostered years earlier. The exit of a key volunteer in prior years, in fact, had been caused by a final detonation she set off intending to settle a turf war once and for all. It goes to show that shotgun riders have great influence over the culture of their ministries and ultimately the church.

Once I realized what we were up against, my team and I decided to try to change the ministry culture through an intentional strategy. We removed the battle over scissors and tape by dedicating one cabinet in each room for communal supplies. We made sure each of the ministries knew they were free to use the supplies under two conditions—that they put them back when they were finished and that they let us know when a particular item ran out so we could restock. It seems so silly looking back, and it took some time for the culture to change, but eventually suspicion and turf wars were traded in for generosity and cooperation. This is what I call the trickle-down rule of leadership. In Luke 6:40 we are told that a student, when fully taught, will be like his teacher. Ultimately, we determine the culture of our ministry through our own attitudes and actions.

This situation taught me one of the greatest lessons of leadership: that mistrust breeds mistrust, and trust breeds trust. Wise team leaders know how to build trust among their team. They know that if their team feels that they can trust them, they will return that trust and also be more likely to build it with others.

Several elements can destroy trust in a team. It's important to know what they are so we can spot them when they arise and cut them off at the root!

Political maneuvering. I've always been a big fan of getting all of your cards out on the table. If your team partners are always mistrusting your next move, they will be driven into one of two postures. Either they will begin to play politics along with you and become your competition, or they will simply shut down in frustration. One thing is for sure: they will not be transparent with you if they see you as their competition.

Putting self above the team. I once served on a staff where one of our team members was always conniving and maneuvering and backstabbing the rest of us. Any time he was in the room, the air was thick with tension.

Everyone in the room, including me, was set on edge and on guard and protecting their own turf. We felt that there was no other way but to play the same games in order to get anything done. It didn't take long to realize the effect of one bad apple on the rest. Self-interest destroys trust and teamwork.

Competition for funding. One great destroyer of trust is competition, especially over funding. It's my position that a staff ought to agree together on projects when funding is an issue (and this is a reality in most churches post 9/11 and the economic downturn). I once served in a church where staff members were forced to compete with each other over the funding of their particular budgets. Team members would try to sneak projects and agendas into hidden places in their budget areas and often tried to beat one another to the punch during planning sessions for the coming year.

At one church, one of the staff would come to the table with excessive funding in various lines of his budget. Then when we were asked to trim the budget to a more manageable size, he would readily offer up his pre-arranged sacrifice and nothing more. This seemingly small act was evidence of self-interest and created mistrust. Those of us who came to the table without fat built in would feel a pinch. An unhealthy silence was always brewing in meetings where finances were being discussed. A staff must be intentional about building trust in this area.

Leadership voids. Trust can become an issue when a leader doesn't lead. When there is a vacuum of leadership, team members are forced to compete over projects and agendas. I'm convinced that there can be little cooperation or consensus in a team where a leader doesn't have his or her sights on the big picture. In a staff environment like this, team members must fight even harder to maintain a sense of team play.

Hidden agendas. Hidden agendas are also huge destroyers of trust. There are legitimate reasons to keep certain plans and projects quiet, but secret motives will almost always erode trust. On one elder board, the chairman of the board would occasionally write into the meeting agenda the words, "Hidden Agenda Items." This was done in a spirit of humor, but it came as a result of a bad experience on another church board where the chairman was regularly bombarded with hidden agenda items from a mean-spirited board member. As I mentioned earlier, I like to have all the cards on the table. This builds trust and makes a safe environment for forward movement. A wise team leader can head off hidden agendas by encouraging team members to get their items in ahead of time so they can be written into the meeting agenda.

A wise leader will learn to build consensus and give the team reasons to trust. I heard about one staff team where a senior pastor would discuss an issue by first asking each team member to express his or her feelings about it. His next move was to use that information against them as he moved forward pursuing his own agenda. Over time, his team learned to keep their opinions to themselves. Blindsiding your team will destroy trust.

Change resistance. On one staff I heard about several younger staff members finding themselves in a situation where the younger people of the church wanted to move forward and grow but felt that the older leadership would not let go of the reins. This challenge carried over into staff relationships. In order to keep important issues at the forefront, the younger leaders would agree to speak in unison at staff and board meetings on key issues. This was all done in a loving, nondivisive spirit. If they ran up against a wall on a particular issue, they would agree not to cause dissension but to continue expressing their desires about the issue and move on to other concerns. Sometimes this team-within-the-team met with success and sometimes they met with failure, but their strategy gave them the sense that they had a voice.

Some of the younger leaders on one of the staffs on which I served became concerned over the disrepair and disheveled appearance of some of the classrooms and common areas of the church. We felt like this was a deterrent to visitors and showed a lack of concern for our guests. We made it a point not to make an issue of this, but we did take action. Each week after our staff meeting we would pick a room or common area and get after it. Room by room, the church started to take on a renewed appearance, and after some time even those who were in charge of the building upkeep got excited about our work and joined in by allocating money for paint and carpet. To this day no one outside our group knows who was responsible for this work, but we did make a difference by forming this team. The point is that sometimes you have to form a group of concerned stakeholders and just get after it.

Perhaps you want to create a list of agenda items. Agree ahead of time when you want to bring these items up for the attention of those who hold the power. One thing you want to be sure to do is agree not to be divisive or manipulative but to move forward in a spirit of love. If you run up against a wall, agree to spend more time praying about the issue, but still use subsequent opportunities to keep the item at the forefront.

Careless words. When I was first a youth pastor, I used to horse around with the kids, and sometimes we'd get to putting each other down: you know, you're so dumb, your momma's so ugly, and so on. An older, more seasoned youth leader challenged me about this kind of behavior with my students. He suggested that I rethink this kind of horsing around, suggesting that I should take on the role of the guardian of our group image. He challenged me to put an end to the putdowns and careless joking. At the time I didn't take him too seriously, but not long after that the guys and I were hanging out in the office, and we got to poking at each other's masculinity as boys sometimes do. I noticed that one of the young men became rather dispirited. Later I pulled him aside to inquire what was wrong, and he took the opportunity to unload a raging battle over his sexual identity.

I vowed that night to take heed of my mentor's wisdom. I put an immediate end to the reckless talk. I began to challenge my students to care for one another by saying only the things that would build each other up. After all, isn't this a biblical concept? We started playing a game called "9." Anytime someone put another student down, someone in the group would blurt out, "Nine!", reminding them that psychologists say it takes nine compliments to restore a person's emotional state after a putdown.

Our students began to feel differently about our group. A deeper love and care for one another began to grow. Students began to bring their friends—something that hadn't happened much before this. Our youth group soon became the place to be on a Sunday night in that town. We didn't change any of our programming or add any fun new events. The only thing that changed was the way we interacted with one another. Mistrust breeds mistrust and trust builds trust in a way that is attractive. No matter your position on your staff or team, make it your goal to be a trust builder with your peers. Remember the trust fall we used to do when we were kids. We'd stand behind someone and tell them to fall straight back, and we'd catch them just before they hit the floor. The whole idea is about trusting the person to catch you. You should be able to have that kind of trust with your team. Your team should know that they are safe with you and your staff. Make it your goal to build trust with your team, and it will be returned to you.

Any leadership team that wants to build a trust-filled environment must value consensus over personal politics. Building consensus is also a way to build trust among team members because it invites everyone along for the ride. Politicking may be a way to get your own agenda accomplished, but it will alienate your peers in the process. There is a place for speaking to the needs or causes that are only important to yourself and your ministry, but if you value teamwork then you must value consensus above your own wishes. When there is trust and teamwork among shotgun riders, there's no telling how far a team can go.

COMMUNICATING CLEARLY

Maybe you're like me, and reading the title of this section has already set you on edge. I have to be honest here: I'm not exactly the poster boy for clear communication. I don't enjoy the subject, and it's never been something I've looked forward to when it needs to happen. And as it turns out, I'm not alone. It's a common experience that those who make a life of communicating God's Word often struggle with communicating plans or the details of upcoming events. But that's no excuse for us not to work at it. If we want to build a team that works well together, communication is essential.

Every Monday on our staff meeting agenda there is an item called "Website Updates." This is where we are encouraged to make sure our section of the website is up-to-date and contains fresh information regarding coming events. I see the looks in the other's eyes around the table with me. They've already been to the church website three times that morning, and everything on their pages is bright and fresh and looking spiffy. I do communicate, and I do try to do it well. It's just that for me it's not something I generally enjoy.

What I've learned about communication has come through difficulties and some pain. I gladly share it with you because I know that I'm not alone here, and I know this subject is the pitfall of many good shotgun riders. More than anything else, I try to go the extra mile in communicating when I feel like it's lacking from the top. A wise leader will use a communication breakdown or weakness as an opportunity to clarify for others about events and other issues.

Communicating in conflict. One of the greatest communication needs happens in ministry at exactly the time when most of us want to crawl in a hole and hide: when there is a conflict. When there is a conflict with a ministry peer or with one of my leaders, everything in me wants to take the fetal position. I have learned through difficulties to take the road that, at first, looks more difficult: to assume the lead in communicating and getting the conflict resolved. These simple steps will help you arrive at the backside of a conflict with a win-win resolution.

The first thing I would advise you to do in this situation is change your role. Generally when there is a conflict there are two sides, and initially we find ourselves on one side of a disagreement. The greatest secret to being good at resolving conflicts is in changing your role.

When someone comes to us with an accusation about one of our programs or something we've done, we immediately want to defend ourselves and the things in which we've invested. We might try to build a support base of others who agree with us and bring this support to bear in discussing the issue with our supposed adversary. This defensive position is actually counterproductive, and I can tell you from experience that you can win the argument and lose the battle or you can win the battle and sacrifice your need to be right. The choice is yours, but if you want a winning solution for your ministry, you must resist every inclination to defend yourself and take your opponent down. The enemy is not your perceived adversary but the evil one who desires to destroy your ministry and foment disharmony.

So how do you change your role? Instead of seeing yourself as being on one side of the argument, see yourself as the leader in getting this conflict resolved—in other words, change your position from combatant to peacemaker. This involves a great amount of careful listening and sometimes a supernatural level of self-control. This is especially true the first few times you try this approach! But the results are well worth it. In those times when you are not able to get out of your role of being at odds with the other party, it will be necessary to have a trusted partner take the leadership role for you.

I am well aware that many of you reading this are going to have the proverbial Type A personality. How do I know this? Because ministry attracts those who aspire to lead, and leaders are generally Type A personalities. If this is you, what I'm saying is going to seem especially foreign. And when you first attempt this, it will feel especially foreign to you. We love to tout our ability to lead and the driven character of our makeup, but a Type A personality may actually be a hurdle to resolving conflict. So get over your need to win an argument or conflict and change your role. Learn to listen deeply and care more about the concerns of others.

There are three vital steps of action to take as you get yourself into the role of peacemaker. First, show them that you are listening by repeating back to them what you hear them saying. For instance, "What I hear you saying is that you feel like we are not watching your child very well because he says that he is picked on by the other kids in his Sunday school class. Is that what you're saying?"

When my wife and I were first married, someone sent us to a marriage workshop where this technique was taught. At first I laughed, thinking how ridiculous it sounded as we took turns and one by one the couples in the room practiced listening to each other. But when we first did this in a real-life conflict, it was amazing how much more quickly we were able to get to a point of understanding the other's perspective. We even began to feel like there was a new level of care and intimacy between us.

A word of caution is needed here: only bring up your side of the issue or your own wounds or offenses after you have listened very carefully and thoroughly to the other's concerns. A person with whom we are having a conflict will almost always sense it if we are only waiting for an opportunity to get our point across. People generally know when we're not listening with our hearts.

Second, make apologies when necessary. If something has happened that involves someone being wronged, then ask that person directly if they will forgive you. This is not always the easiest thing to do. At times the party we offend will be unforgiving or unyielding. I was once in charge of a Saturday basketball event for boys. I made the announcement that the event would be cancelled the week before. One of the students was out of the room at the time, and he rode his bike several miles into town that Saturday only to find the church empty and no one around. The parents were quite upset and demanded that I come to their home to explain how this had happened. When I got there I explained what had happened and apologized. At that point they took it upon themselves to unload on me. They called my actions unforgiveable and would not bend. I was unable to regain their favor in any way. It wasn't until years later that they actually said they might have been too harsh on their young youth leader.

We must remember that our responsibility is not to earn another's forgiveness but only to ask for it when necessary. The granting of forgiveness is really between the other person and their Creator. No doubt it's frustrating and hurtful when, after a conflict with someone, you apologize for your wrongs and the other person doesn't acknowledge their own part in the conflict. At this point we usually feel like taking our apology back. When you work with people, conflicts are going to be inevitable, and working in a church doesn't change that—in fact, we could probably make a strong case that conflict is going to be more likely in a church because our enemy is so angry about our agenda.

Third, attend to their concern. If you can, do something about what they are concerned about. Don't just say you're sorry that they're upset. Try to find something to do that will show them that you care deeply about their concern. Help them with whatever it is that has them irritated. I once had a mom call me to complain about the start time of an event that made it difficult for her to get her children into our child care program and then get to her class, which started fifteen minutes before the child-care doors opened. I listened carefully to her concern and assured her that this was important to us. Then I made special arrangements for her children to be cared for by someone in our ministry. Her real concern was that she couldn't get to her Bible study until after it had actually begun. I did what I could to rectify the situation.

I once had a couple come to me quite angry because they thought their child had been "nearly molested" by one of our volunteers. I asked them if we could meet together so I could hear their concern. When I met with them, what I learned had actually happened was that our volunteer had teased their daughter by lightly tugging on her ponytail. I also learned that they had shared their concern with two other leaders before working their way up to me.

This couple was seriously angry about the incident and was considering a lawsuit against the church. After meeting with several eyewitnesses, I learned that nothing like a molestation had actually happened. But after I met with them, they thanked me, indicating that they finally felt like their concern had been heard. All I really did was listen, then meet with my leaders to investigate and reaffirm our policies related to our conduct with children. After that, I sent a letter to the couple telling them how I had followed up and thanked them for bringing their concern to me. The thing that made the difference was that someone had finally listened to their concern and followed up with it. Remember that the goal is not to win the battle but to accomplish peace and further our ministry and the gospel.

Real care will almost always involve some kind of action. Yes, there are times when people just need someone to listen to them, but often when there is a conflict, only some sort of action will communicate that you care. A wise leader will assure those who bring them concerns that they care about their concern and will show their care with action.

Lastly, I always send a note to anyone who comes to me with a concern, whether that concern has to do with my own actions or with one of the ministries I oversee. This is one thing you can do that will be appropriate in any conflict, whether or not any other specific action is required. In that note, as I did with the couple who felt that their daughter had been treated improperly, I simply review what their concern was as I understand it, and then I reiterate anything I have committed to do as a result of our conversation. This kind of note will communicate that you care, and it seals up your role as taking charge of the resolution process. Usually what most people want is to be heard and understood. They want to feel like you care about them deeply.

I always close the note by asking if I've missed anything from our conversation or if there's anything I misinterpreted or misrepresented. That way there can never be an accusation that I twisted someone's words, and it gives the other person an opportunity to express anything further.

After I began to take this approach, I started to see a new level of confidence in the people I work with. I don't see myself as particularly gifted in the area of conflict resolution, but I have heard some of the people I've helped through conflict say they felt I was approachable and caring. Following these three simple steps won't help you win an argument, but they will help you gain the trust of your constituents.

Of course, if you do these three things, there are no guarantees that the outcome will be automatic peace. Conflict resolution, when done well, is a process—not a switch you can flip. You must stop defending yourself and trying to give your own perspective and start listening with your heart— hearing what someone is saying by getting in touch with the things they care about.

SAYING THANK YOU

One of the most important facets of building an effective team is saying thank you. People who serve in your ministry want to know that their service is recognized by you. I know we can argue that it only matters that Jesus sees, but the truth is we're all human, and it makes it so much more fun to serve when the leader appreciates it!

I've heard well-meaning shotgun riders argue that they don't want to go overboard with this, giving volunteers the idea that they are serving them instead of serving Christ. There is a way to make the point to your people that they are ultimately serving God but still show them that you appreciate their service. Sometimes I'll say something like, "I know you could serve God other places in the church, and I appreciate that you're serving him here." This lets them know that ultimately they're serving God, not you, and still shows them that you appreciate what they're doing.

Thanking people also keeps our own perspective about them in the right place. I don't like to use the word "volunteers." It just doesn't seem fitting for what is supposed to be an act of worship. I now call them partners. Further, I don't call what they do volunteering. I call it serving. I don't want to diminish their acts of worship, of serving God, to something more like what I sign up to do at my kids' school. I want to encourage service in ministry by calling it what it should be: an act of worship, a way to say to Jesus, "Thank you for all you've done for me, let my service be a way to love you."

Our partners need to know that we appreciate what they do. On Sunday morning and Wednesday evening during our midweek kids' program, I try to wander the hallways and thank those who serve. I try to be as specific as possible. I'll say, "Thanks for always being on time." Or "I really appreciate the way you communicate love to your students." I also ask them if they need any help in their area. I've built my ministry in such a way as to make myself available to help where I'm needed. After you practice these habits of verbally saying thank you and being available, you'll find that you don't have to verbalize your thanks every week. Just your presence says that you appreciate them.

Another way you can say thank you is through gifts. I have built up some funds in a couple of areas in my budget lines over the years for the purpose of giving gifts and thank-yous to leaders. I try to give a nice thank-you gift to each of my unpaid program leaders at the end of their ministry season. Of course it's the thought that counts, but I try to make the gift significant enough to communicate that I really appreciate what they're doing. I like to give my leaders gift certificates to nicer local restaurants and make the amount enough that they can take their spouse along and have a nice date night. Oftentimes the spouse of a ministry leader can be overlooked, and yet they also contribute to our ministry by sharing their spouse with us. Sometimes smaller gifts like movie passes or gift certificates for coffee or ice cream shops are a convenient way to say thanks to those who serve.

At Christmastime, I try to give gifts to all the leaders and directors who report directly to me. We serve in a very financially conservative environment, and when I came, I found it strange that very few gifts were exchanged between friends or work associates around Christmas. This carried over into our church environment. I began to give gifts to my key leaders each year, and over time I've noticed that many of them are now giving gifts to volunteers in their own areas. Gift giving is a way of saying "I appreciate you," and it can be contagious.

There are also ways to give meaningful gifts without spending a ton of money. Each year our pastoral staff makes homemade goodies for Christmas baskets to be given to each member of our office staff. We each make some kind of Christmas cookies or baked goods. A person in the church packages our creations in large cellophane-wrapped gift baskets, and we present them to our staff at our Christmas party.

Finding ways to say thank you is so important. There are many ways to do this so that our leaders know that we care about them and appreciate what they do. These are ways we also create a fun environment for people to serve. Ultimately, none of us is alone in ministry. We are riding alongside others, and the more we can do to make that ride a pleasant, fruitful, and successful one, the better.

CHAPTER SIX

WORKING THE SYSTEM

I once served in a little church where a man had died and left the church $500,000. I was asked to lead a team that was to decide what should be done with the funds, and I felt honored to be given such a responsibility. Once underway, our team asked the church members for ideas, held times of prayer together, and looked for guidance from the family of the deceased. We came up with a list of twenty or so items we felt would make a difference for the kingdom, and the elders endorsed our plan to begin at the top of the list and work our way down. The list included everything from the hiring of new staff to building improvements. Excitement ran high as we anticipated seeing important changes happen.

Sitting in the back of the room during a subsequent all-church meeting, I watched helplessly as one of the church power brokers stood up and made a brief case for using about one-fourth of the funds for a new bus. He had a friend who owned a bus company looking to upgrade their equipment, and he wondered if the church would want to purchase one of their old buses. A number of those up the political power chain spoke in favor of the move, and the item passed by a small margin. Several on our team protested, asking why we weren't going to honor what the team had done. I felt railroaded, and in frustration my team refused to meet again. I couldn't blame them.

Many shotgun riders are intimidated by the forms of church governance. Especially if we are young, church leadership structures may look cumbersome and given to bureaucracy to us. Often the temptation is to give up and back off, and yet this is counterproductive. There needs to be a better way.

Shotgun riders will do well to come to terms with the way things are. We need to find a way of relating to those who wield the power and control so things get done—so things that matter for the future get done. Chances are you resonate with what I'm saying, but you're burned out or trampled down or at a loss to know what to do next. I trust in the pages that follow you will find the help you are looking for.

Your Make-or-Break Opportunity

As a shotgun rider, you are in a make-or-break position. You can save the day for the church or you can bring it down. Some would argue the senior pastor is the one who holds the bulk of visionary power in the church, and this is somewhat true, but consider this: If a church has a dynamic senior pastor who is a visionary leader and communicates well, but the shotgun riders do not support or follow him, the church will go nowhere. Conversely, a church with poor leadership from the top can still move forward and grow if the shotgun riders bring wise individual leadership and cooperative collaboration.

You are in a significant position to carry your church through, even during difficult times. If the stagecoach driver gets incapacitated or is unable to carry on, the shotgun rider must use his position to help guide the precious cargo and passengers in safe travel.

Please understand that I'm not advocating a hostile takeover—and without question, this happens. I know of a church where an associate convinced the senior pastor in a moment of vulnerability to step down and subsequently ended up in his role. He is still in that spot over twenty years later, but I can't say the evidence shows that God's blessing ever joined in the venture. I have been in that same position myself, and I chose to honor the leadership God put in place. I believe this is always the right course unless there is some major sin issue or a serious abuse of power involved.

I understand what it's like to know you could easily start a new work with your own followers. In my own case, a number of my loyal, albeit angry, partners in ministry asked me to start a new church, promising their allegiance and support. I couldn't do it. Not because I didn't want to, but because God wouldn't let me, and I was sure it wouldn't honor him. These kinds of church plants rarely go well in the long run.

So no, I would never recommend any act that fosters dissention in any way, and I don't think God generally blesses those kinds of activities. What I'm talking about is standing in the gap where you're needed and honoring God by providing godly leadership without expectation. Matthew 6:33 tells us to seek God's kingdom first and all these things will be added unto us. Don't seek after a place of leadership that isn't yours. Don't seek followers and the acclamation of men. Don't seek after all these things: seek his kingdom and his righteousness, and let him worry about the rest.

In 1 Samuel 24 and 26, we read two stories that illustrate how important it is to honor the person whom God has placed in a position of authority. In 1 Samuel 16, David was chosen by God to be Israel's next king, but Saul was still king for a time, and he began to despise David. His disdain drove him to set out on a mission to kill David, but God protected him. On two occasions David had opportunities to kill Saul and didn't. When others questioned his decision not to harm Saul, David said, "I will not stretch out my hand against…the Lord's anointed." David exhibited complete trust in God and his timing.

Follow this logic. If God is the one who ultimately puts leaders in place, then how did those up the chain come into their positions? They are there because God put them there or because he allows them to remain. Too much time is wasted in criticism of church leaders. Yes, there are ways to handle disagreements, and yes, problems should be addressed; and I hope you find yourself in a staff atmosphere where disagreements and concerns can be handled appropriately. (If you don't, you might want to consider finding one where they can.)

WORKING THE SYSTEM

Many churches today, even many progressive ones, are still operating with antiquated decision-making systems left over from the previous era. Often, for the shotgun rider, there is little hope of changing these structures. So we learn to operate within them until we are in a position to make changes. One of the greatest snags for young leaders is knowing how to work the systems of traditional decision-making in order to get things done. Many feel either pressured to use manipulative measures or play political games. On the other extreme is the feeling of just wanting to give up. Even though the decision-making structures of your church might not be as you would have designed them, you can find your way through with a little help. I have spent the better part of my ministry career working with these systems, and I can assure you that things can get done.

It might help to change the way you look at the hurdle in front of you. Working the system is more like a dance than like a negotiation or a debate. I get a kick out of watching the British House of Commons debate issues. On our cable system, there is a channel that regularly plays these debates. The two parties sit in opposing galleys in relatively close proximity, facing each other. Various speakers will address the other side in face-to-face arguments that are often direct and in the other's face and many times includes finger pointing and raised voices. Speakers are often interrupted by thunderous shouts and boos. I'm always amused by this, and I can't help but think that some churches spend the bulk of their time debating like this and little time actually accomplishing much of anything.

We must realize that working the system is not like winning a debate, or even like sitting at a negotiation table. Working the system must be like a dance, where you delicately and enjoyably move through the discussion with grace and ease. We must be the partner with whom others want to dance. We must be the sought-after dancer who knows how to glide through each issue without dropping our partner.

When approaching decisions, wise shotgun riders will avoid making others feel less important because of their views or disagreement with them. At the same time we must be direct, especially when dealing with important matters that affect the growth and vitality of the church. I once was called on to speak to an issue in our church's deacon meeting. I had prepared a short address with several points that backed up what I was saying. Going in, I had the sense that there was opposition to the issue, and no sooner had I started speaking than one well-meaning deacon, one of the good ol' boys, interrupted by saying, "What's the point here?" His words sent me into a fit of stage fright I hadn't experienced since the fifth grade. After bumbling through the remainder of my thoughts, I sat down feeling defeated.

Since that time, whenever I have to address that group, I go into the meeting with a determination to playfully but firmly include that man and others of his ilk in my presentation. Sometimes when you play their game, you can earn their respect and get your points heard. I might say something like, "Now I know Darrel will have something to say on this matter, and I'm sure he'll let me speak my mind and hear me through first." Sometimes you have to play the game even though it seems out of place or out of date. It's the nature of the dance.

Over the years, I have learned many other keys to working the system. *Building bridges.* When you're required to make a presentation, you may want to look at it as an opportunity to build bridges. Building trust and acceptance may require more time and patience than just pushing for your own way, and you may need to wait for others to cross those bridges at a later time and at their own will. But the other, more frustrating, option is to try to plow headlong into issues with the goal of achieving an agenda at all costs. When we do, we often end up building walls that no one wants to scale. It is said that more flies are attracted with honey than with vinegar, and this applies in the business of the church as well as anywhere else.

I have a friend who was a very likeable youth pastor on staff at a nearby church. Generally youth pastors are not thought of as change-makers for the church as a whole, but I also know that way of thinking is wrong-headed. After all, who is shaping the minds of the next generation of leaders? My friend's senior pastor moved on to take a position elsewhere, and the church hired him as their new senior pastor. In just a few short years, he was able to make some incredible changes, and the church began to grow. Was this because he was good at convincing people of his agenda? No, he really wasn't that articulate. He had simply laid the groundwork through years of building relationships with the people God had called him to serve as an associate.

I have seen this same scenario play out in many churches and with numerous people. An influential person isn't always the most convincing or even the most articulate; sometimes he or she is simply the best friend or the most caring individual.

Honest, open communication. One of the qualities of a good leader is honest communication. If we are to see change take root, we will do well to speak the truth in love. We must get to the point and speak what God has put on our hearts, but we must do it in love. When a board member speaks harshly in a meeting, we must say, "I know you feel passionately about this, but you may want to consider communicating your views in a way that is less offensive." When a teacher or leader shows up late, voice your concern in love: "Joe, I really appreciate your desire to teach, but when you're late, the parents of these children get frustrated because they want to get to their class too."

Sometimes we find ourselves feeling uneasy about a decision on our staff team. We might feel uncomfortable speaking honestly with those who are up the chain, but it's vitally important that we voice what we're sensing. Even when we can't put into words how we feel about something, it's good to voice our discomfort. Try saying, "I don't know why I feel uneasy about this decision, but since I first heard the idea, I have felt uncomfortable with it." Sometimes just getting your concern on the table is enough to get the team to rethink things.

Maybe you're like me, and you find confrontation of any kind challenging. I've had to learn the hard way that conflict-avoidant behaviors only make difficult situations more difficult. You might tend to leave confrontation to others who seem to be better at it, perhaps someone up the leadership chain. You might feel like you're just not the right person for the job. My experience tells me that just the opposite is true. The person who tends to rush into conflict headfirst will many times just make the situation worse. The leader who is reluctant to address issues may actually handle them more carefully and with a greater desire to communicate love.

When I'm facing a conflict and I want to run away, I've learned to try to say something small—something that helps open the door for further discussion but doesn't create a big blowup. Saying something is usually better than saying nothing. So if a teacher is rushing past me on a Sunday morning, late again to his class, I might say, "I know you're running late; maybe we could just talk about it later." This says I notice you're late, but it opens the door to talk further at a time when the teacher is not quite as likely to explode in frustration. When your tendency is to say nothing, say something. It will actually pave the way to having constructive discussions at a later point.

Too often, younger staff members feel that they have no voice, and they choose to sit silent in staff or board meetings. This is counterproductive. If you want to see your church keep current, then someone who *is* current needs to speak. A healthy, functioning staff team will be in the habit of listening to the wisdom of each team member. Obviously, the buck needs to stop somewhere—usually with the senior pastor on a staff—and the team needs to respect decisions that are made by its leaders, but a good leader will listen to the wisdom of all its members.

When this dynamic is not present, it's often felt most keenly by the team's newest and youngest members. Perhaps this is you. If it is, it may be up to you to speak to this issue and try to get the attention of the senior leaders. Try saying, "I'm not sure if you want to hear from me on this issue, I know I'm new here, but I wonder if there is another way to approach this."

Being a team player. We've already discussed this issue at length, but it bears repeating here. When I was in college, I played a lot of intermural sports with the guys from my floor. My roommate Don used to say he liked basketball especially because it was a picture of how you played in life. I've observed that you can have a team of average players who excel because they just play team ball really well. You can also have a team full of hotshots who can slam dunk and make three-pointers, but if they don't play team ball, they won't be long-term winners.

Making your words count. I was a youth pastor for so many years that certain verses are just always with me. One that has stuck is, "Don't let anyone look down on you because you are young but set an example for the believers in; speech, life, love, faith and purity" (1 Timothy 4:12). Why did Paul write these words to Timothy? Because when you're young, others tend not to give you the respect you should have. This may be apparent in your staff meetings or your church board meetings. You may even at times feel railroaded by those with more years behind them. So what are you to do about this?

We are told to not give others any reason to look down on us. One of the specific areas mentioned is our speech. I have had to learn this the hard way, as I tend to run my mouth. I have learned that when you're always the first to speak to issues, people tend not to listen. When you have something to say about every issue, what you say has less impact and meaning. So what's the cure? Speak less. After all, being slow to speak and quick to listen is a biblical concept (James 1:19). Try to speak less often, and when you do speak, have something to say that is thought-out. Unless you're in a think-tank environment, constantly thinking out loud will only cause others to tune you out.

Sometimes, to keep myself out of talking mode I will turn to someone in the room who hasn't spoken and say, "Joe, what are your thoughts on this? We haven't heard from you yet." This makes the point that I want to hear from others. It also says I don't need to be the only one to speak, and it communicates to everyone at the table that I care what they think.

Of course, there are times when you just have to speak to a particular issue. There are indeed hills worth dying on; you just want to make sure that you've chosen the hill. Don't let the battles pick you. As you and others who share your concern for the church meet together, you will want to agree together regarding which hills you will battle on. At the church where I now serve, we are discussing the possibility of a new welcome center. When the issue comes up, there are several of us who speak in unison. As questions about it are brought to us, we support one another and communicate a unified voice. Remember that a cord of three strands is not easily broken.

Build from the positives. It's always best to build from your strengths in any endeavor. When something is done well in your circle of influence, it's important to highlight it. Come to your staff or team meeting with a praise of something you've seen that was done right or well. I've heard it said that people don't do what you expect; they do what you inspect. I believe this is wrong-headed, because people really do respond to genuine positive encouragement. I've seen this truth evidenced in my years of work with volunteers.

Too much time in ministry is wasted talking about the bads. A friend of mine who built a large real-estate company outside of Chicago used to say, "The bads are bad for business." I think this runs true in ministry as well. If people are saying bad things about your church, then that is the reputation it will have in your community. I suppose you could just pay your staff and volunteers a commission each time they registered one positive comment about your ministry or church, but that wouldn't really be genuine, would it? The key is that the positive talk must be genuine. It grows from a combination of caring relationships and shared common beliefs. It is built from the inside out more than the outside in.

When people know that you genuinely care about them, and when they believe in the goals and direction of your ministry, positive feelings and comments will grow. That positive talk and energy will communicate to those who attend your programs and then will be spread throughout your community. This is an attractive force many times greater than any advertising campaign in which your church could ever embark. Conversely, negative talk and feelings will also spread through your staff and out to your community at the same rate.

Communicate truth. Make your goal when communicating to be more about truth than winning a particular agenda item. This strikes at the heart of what it means to be pastoral. I mentioned that right now my church is talking about the possibility of undertaking a building program. I could go into meetings with guns blazing. The staff and I could battle hard for the space we want added to our building, and we just might be convincing enough to get it. The real issue driving this possibility, though, is not so much the need for new space as much as it is that we need better ways of welcoming visitors, and we need to create environments for fellowship. If the powers that be come up with alternative ways of making this happen in our current space, then we have accomplished a great thing.

So when we have the opportunity to communicate about this issue, we talk about the truth that we need to create avenues for fellowship and a welcoming environment for visitors. The concept we keep in front of people is not so much that we need new space, although I'll be surprised if another way can be found, but that we need better ways to welcome people. Don't be one to drive in a stake on every issue and fight for your agenda. Instead, be about communicating truth. I find that people generally respond to truth. A wise shotgun rider will trust that people know what to do and how to respond when they are presented with the facts. Remember that trust builds trust and mistrust builds mistrust.

Engage the machinists. At the beginning of this book, I mentioned that ministry has changed enormously in the last generation, and the change continues. Because the landscape has changed so much, a new resilience is required. We can no longer afford to simply ride the wave as sometimes has been done. The machinery left over from the previous generation may indeed be cranking along, still oiled and maintained by those who built it, but we can no longer afford to ride old machinery and allow old ways of doing ministry to direct us. If we do, we run the danger of being driven into nonexistence through cultural irrelevance. In many cases, younger staff members can see this clearly—but there's still an old guard in place, people who built the systems that are still in place. How are we to effectively engage with them? I bought an antique tractor about the time we were building our current home. I knew that we would be planting trees and doing some heavy landscaping as well as planting the grass around the house, so I thought it would be a good investment, and I knew I could sell the tractor when I was finished with it. It was a great way to save on all the work we needed done, but there was one problem: that old tractor constantly needed work. It seemed about every time I went to use it, I had to repair something else before I could get the real work started. Old machines are great to look at but require extra work to keep running.

Over time, it is common for those who build great machinery to forget why their machines were created and engage themselves with the task of keeping the machinery running. Sometimes this happens long after the needs which drove them to build their machines have changed or are gone. Keeping the system running can become the meaning of their existence and the blight of those who follow. Much energy can be given over the issue of machinery maintenance, and this can be the undoing of both those who desire to keep their equipment running and of those who follow them.

Oftentimes, those who built and maintain these machines waste too much energy trying to get younger folks to help them revitalize their equipment. Perhaps you've heard the question, "What can we do to get the younger people out to this event?" Or "Do you think we can get the students to sit down front?" These might seem like important questions, but they are the wrong questions, and they're directed at the wrong people. A better approach for leaders is to ask of themselves, "What can we do to be the kind of ministry in which the young people want to participate?" And lest we think we're faultless in the matter, know that those of us who come after the Great Era bear responsibility, for we have spent too much time and energy either in disputing the value of what seemed to us antiquated or in spending our energy trying to keep old forms running. I believe there is a better way.

We must engage those who are busy at the old machines, for they are fading from our midst. We must get those who are holding the wrenches and the oil cans to help us. Not by showing us what techniques and parameters are required to keep the machinery clicking along. No, we must discover from them the passion that caused them to build their machines in the first place. For what important causes was their machinery built, and what great societal needs drove them to build such apparatuses? These are the discussions that get overlooked because we're too busy fighting over the machines.

As I write this chapter, I'm sitting in a small concrete room in Guatemala City. I've just come down from a mountain village ten hours away where there is no running water and little that resembles home. Why am I here? Because Casey, the youth guy at my church, is thinking about bringing his youth group here this summer for a mission trip and wanted me to come along to check it out, and because I finally decided to come visit the village where an older woman from my church served as a missionary to a remote people group.

For ten years, I've heard Jean tell stories about the work she did with her husband (who has now gone to heaven). She tells them at Vacation Bible School and at our missions conference. I have to confess there have been times when I've thought, *Not again. Not another missionary story.* Jean is eighty-two, and she's as tough as nails. She doesn't seem like eighty-two— more like thirty-two and full of spunk and life. She's always positive and looking forward, always smiling and cheerful. Without question, Jean is at her machine, just months away from completing her life's work: the translation of the Bible into the Popti language.

My church is full of Jeans. Lots of older folks with smiles and friendly greetings. To be honest, I hardly know most of them. Jean I know because she comes to VBS and tells her missionary stories. But just yesterday, my view of Jean came undone. She's no longer another sweet old lady at my church; she's my friend. I was standing on a concrete slab on top of a fog-covered mountain—just another slab on a vacant lot at another dot out there on the mission field. As Maria, the pastor's wife, told us about plans for a school to be built on this site, I kept wondering how they were going to get this old slab out of the way. I asked her about it, and she grew excited. I could hardly understand her Spanish, and it became incomprehensible as she broke into Popti, the native language. I knew she was trying to tell us something.

As she stood on a stoop that once was the entrance to a building, I understood one thing: "This was Shuwin's front door." Suddenly I realized that Shuwin was *Jean.* Suddenly all of those stories I'd heard made sense. Now I was part of the story. This was Jean's home, the home where they began translating the Bible into the language of the Jaceltec people. This was the slab that once held the home of a missionary family, a home that was burned by guerilla fighters in 1981. I saw a kitchen and I heard children playing. I saw the native people coming and going from Jean's home, I saw them reading from a Bible that Jean and Denny had translated, and I realized that this older lady from my church and her husband were real people.

My heart has done a one-eighty, and I'm embarrassed that I ever rolled my eyes at those missionary stories. Just yesterday I stood on a barren concrete slap on the top of a mountain where a family gave their blood, sweat, and tears to help others know the love of Christ that I daily take for granted.

There are lots of folks at their machines in my church. I'm sure they're in your church too. They're holding the wrenches and the oil cans and doing what they can to maintain the old machinery. Yes, some of the machines are antiquated, but it's not the machinery we need as much as a connection with the saints who run them. If we can get past the discussion about the machinery to see and understand the passion that drove them to build their great machines, we will have gained much.

The Yard-of-the-Month Effect

Numerous things can make the shotgun ride challenging. Many of these are built into the systems we serve under, and many are a result of being in the number-two position. Mismanagement by leadership, an undervaluing of your significant ministry, and personal discontent all play a role. There is another factor I like to call the yard-of-the-month effect.

My wife and I used to take a regular detour through a golf community. We could only dream of living in this particular neighborhood, but it was fun to look at the beautiful homes with their picturesque yards. The home owners association gave out an award for the owners who had made significant improvements to their yard, and they would put a "yard of the month" sign in the yard so all the residents would notice and admire—and I'm sure they did too. All except the guy who lived next door. I always took notice of the neighbors who lived on either side of the winner. I'd make comments to my wife as we'd pass by. "Look at this guy next door with the big dead spot in the middle of his lawn." Or "Check out the weeds around their flowerbeds. Slackers!"

Do you think the nice folks next door were jumping up and down over the neighbor's careful eye for detail? Doubtful! They were thinking about all the things wrong with their own yards and how bad this makes them look. They were probably making a list of things that needed to happen on their property.

Sometimes ministry is like that. If you occasionally get to preach or speak in your pastor's main venue, what is the reaction? If you are gifted in this area, you may get a less than favorable response from your senior pastor—that is, unless you are fortunate enough to serve under a particularly godly and humble leader who is interested in building others up in their ministry abilities, one who is not threatened by other's giftedness.

When I was in college, I attended a large church with numerous staff members. They were in a period of rapid growth, and a lot of hiring was going on. They brought on a number of "experts" to head up various ministry areas. Several of these staff members were well known around the country for their expertise in their respective fields, and we were regularly reminded of this at services. I never could understand why this church, which hired the best staff they could find, would schedule unskilled folks to speak at services while the senior pastor was gone. There were a number of gifted communicators on staff, but they were rarely offered second speaking opportunities. The lead pastor himself was an extremely gifted communicator, but those who were hired to help with the weekend teaching load were—how should I say this nicely?—pathetic!

I remember looking forward to hearing one of the new hires speak. It had been announced several weeks in advance that he had been hired to help with preaching. When the day arrived, I was sadly disappointed. The message was horrible—I struggled to know what exactly he was trying to say. Nothing seemed to make sense. To make matters worse, he said "Oh my God" numerous times throughout his message and used a curse word— one of the biggies. I looked around wondering what the general reaction was. I saw lots of winces and expressions of bewilderment. It made me wonder what they were thinking by putting this man in front of the people. How could a church that had hired such prominent experts for other responsibilities fail so miserably in this one area? Why would they not want to put the best teachers in front of their people? Can a church only have one gifted teacher?

When I came on board at one church, Jeff, the senior pastor, said he was thrilled I could speak and was glad I wanted to. He hadn't had many Sundays out of the pulpit in the few years before my arrival, and it seemed like a great partnership. That is, until one week after my first Sunday on the platform. Outside the offices, I could hear Val, the director of our women's ministry, instructing Jeff on his need to speak "more like Doug." As I rounded the hallway corner, I came face-to-face with Jeff, and his expression communicated volumes. I knew my message had hit home with people by a number of comments I'd heard over the previous week. He wasn't a bad communicator, just different. The awkwardness of that experience remained throughout my tenure.

It's a great privilege for an associate to speak in "big church." It can, however, come at a price for the shotgun rider. You want to do your best. You're not looking to win the sermon-of-the-month award, and you have on your heart to address some things that are important to you. Truth be told, your shotgun seat has afforded you connections with those on the ground floor. This alone may put you in a position to speak in a way that affects people deeply. Then there's the advantage of being a new voice, which is always refreshing. I've always said my speaking would be pretty dry if I had to do it fifty-some weeks every year!

Hopefully you find yourself in a healthy relationship with your senior leader in this area. If so, you will want to cherish what you have in the working relationship you share. It is a rare commodity.

Once as a young pastor I was given the opportunity to speak in "big church." The senior pastor was working his way through a book of the Bible, and I was assigned one of the chapters. I knew I was young and green, so I worked to prepare the message weeks in advance. I wanted to do a good job. I felt good about it afterward, and by the response I received, I thought it had gone well. I was shocked two Sundays later when the senior pastor returned to the platform and repreached my passage. Apparently he thought I had not done an adequate job. I was devastated and took it personally.

Speaking at your church's weekend services can be a catch-22. Do a great job, and you may find favor in the eyes of the people. However, it may not help you in your specific area of ministry, and it may actually point out deficits in your pastor's abilities. Be careful! Always remember, the successes God gives you are from him. And if you have a favorable relationship with your senior pastor and you speak regularly to the congregation, you have a beautiful thing.

In the church where I now serve, I get to speak two or three times each year. Randy, the senior pastor, has generously given me these opportunities, and I value them. Each time I'm in front of the people, I'm aware of the privilege and responsibility given me. Some of today's greatest Bible teachers and speakers have stood in that pulpit: people like Carl Henry, James Boice, Tony Campolo, Elisabeth Elliott, Calvin Miller, and J.I. Packer, to name a few. Nothing like a little pressure! I'm blessed with a humble and godly leader in Randy Faulkner. Without fail, he will call me the day before I speak to let me know he will be praying for me as I teach. It's great to know, and freeing too, that he wants me to do well in this important ministry and that he isn't threatened by sharing the platform with one of his subordinates.

Because of the importance of communicating well given such a great cloud of witnesses, I've started sneaking into the auditorium a few days before I'm to speak for a dry run. This helps ease the tension, and I find I'm better able to relax when I'm up front. A wise shotgun rider will treat these up-front opportunities with high regard.

Follow Your Passions

Working on a staff, within a system, and often around old ways of doing this requires a lot of healthy compromise. We need to learn to honor those in leadership over us and those who came before us. But compromise can go too far, so before I close this chapter, I want to address the topic of following your passions.

After spending way too much time trying to be the person someone else was telling me to be, I finally came to a place of deciding I was going to be who God had created me to be. It's too easy to fall into the trap of trying to be someone you're not. There are way too many voices out there calling us to conform to a mold that isn't ours. It might come from worn-out traditions, from a team leader, or even from a senior pastor. Whatever the source, there's a good chance the pressure to conform has been flying under your radar, slowly squeezing you into something you were never meant to be without you even realizing it.

Perhaps you've decided to try harder, and maybe, just maybe, you feel a fleeting sense that you're gaining on some elusive carrot. You've told yourself the lie that if you just keep striving, one day you'll hear your leader say, "Well done." Or maybe you've already come to realize that the carrot is never going to be enjoyed. You'll never be the person your pastor or team leader hopes you'll aspire to become, and you've accepted that.

At times it's good to ask the question, "Who is your God?" Not in the sense of what is God's character, but who is your god in the sense of what *person* is your god? Is it the person sitting across from you at the staff meeting, or maybe the person conducting your performance review? While it's important to realize that we are called to honor our overseers, we do well to remind ourselves that they are not God. They are not the ones who created you with your unique signature stamp of abilities, talents, and character traits. They are not the ones who called you into service. So take a moment right now and ask yourself, "Who is your God?"

I spent way too much time early in ministry trying to be the pastor others wanted me to be instead of finding satisfaction in being the person I was created to be. After beating my head against the wall for too long, I finally realized that all I got from doing it was a headache. It isn't worth it. I never did enjoy that carrot, I never got the praise I was hoping for, and finally I had to realize I was serving the wrong god. I was trying to please a god who couldn't be pleased because he hadn't created me. More than that, the one I had put in the place of my Father was woefully out of touch with those around him. He didn't have a clue how I had been created, and he hadn't an inkling of who God really intended me to be. Once I realized I was staring into the eyes of a lifeless golden calf, I knew I had some internal work to do. I spent some months asking God to give me back my joy in serving him.

During this time of searching, and through a set of circumstances, I fell into a writing opportunity where I got to influence thousands of people a number of times each month. I still do this, and I do it anonymously: most of the folks at my church don't even know I do it, and I've come not to care. This might not seem that life altering to you, but to me this was huge. Twenty years prior I had thrown in the trash a folder containing some things I had written—things God had put on my heart to share. After hearing some voices telling me my writing wasn't significant or important for pastoral work, I threw my work in the trash and walked away from something I now realize God had wired me to do. For over twenty years I had stuffed away this passion and the vital equipment God had given me to serve him.

Don't ever let your boss define you. Let God define your passions. Settle this early in your ministry if you can. Too many times, old models of ministry or old definitions of what it means to be a pastor or leader get pushed onto younger staff. If you're in that kind of oppressive environment, consider finding a role or position that matches more closely with what God has designed you to be and do.

Follow your passions because they are God-given. *He* created you. God fitted you for his service, so find ways to work within your passions and abilities. Pursue what brings you joy, and perhaps it will become your career. Tell others, especially those up the pipe, what makes you tick and what gets you out of bed each day. Let them know this is what God has built you for.

If you find yourself under the thumb of a small "g" god, get yourself out. You'll never find joy in your ministry if you're not serving the big "G" God. Get on your knees and begin a conversation with your Father. Know that he wants you to have joy in serving him, and he knows exactly what kind of service will be a match for you. If you've lost your way, this is the only method I know that will get your joy back.

So go ahead, follow your passions—the ones God built into you. Don't follow someone else's, follow yours. If God put in you a desire to write, then write for him. If he created you to work with students, then by all means do that. It seems silly to say it as an adult, but it needs to be said: Do what God meant you to do. Do the good works he created you to do, not someone else's good works, or the works someone else is telling you to do (see Ephesians 2:10). You will never find joy if you don't.

The time has come to return to the love of your assignment and the thrill of the ride. Please accept my thoughts as a call to rise above and once again rediscover the intoxicating sense of happiness that was there when you began. Accept this as a charge to return to your love for the adventure of following your God wherever he leads you. Yes, you can find joy in your ministry, and you can thrive and have great fulfillment as you follow in what God has set your hand to do. You, my friend, are the shotgun rider!

CHAPTER SEVEN

SPITTING, SPLITTING AND QUITTING
(OR JUST GETTING FIRED)

Sitting there motionless with my jaw hanging open, I was too confused, too frozen over for any one emotion to rise to the surface. His words pierced. *This can't be happening,* I thought; *he can't really mean what he's saying.* The letter Jay handed me gave a brief explanation of the decision and a vague reference to the possibility of a couple of months' severance if I cooperated. He said there was a meeting set up with two of the elders the next morning, where they would explain in further detail the reasoning behind their decision and answer any questions I might have. "You'll thank me later," he said, "this will actually be a good thing." The spin was hardly convincing; even he didn't look like he believed it. He stood to leave, emotionless as a stranger.

I was stunned, unable to move, clenching the letter for what seemed an eternity. I wanted to squeeze it into nonexistence. I'd had no idea there was even a problem, having had my annual review just a few weeks prior— when Jay had given me high marks in every area. Could he not have explained at that time if there was an issue? Now what was I to do? How would I ever find a new ministry position with this black eye? How could I be so stupid as to allow this to happen to me, to my reputation, to my wife and my family? What signs had I missed?

I couldn't find the strength to pry myself from my chair, but I knew I had to go home and tell Juli. What would I say? How would she respond? Would she be angry, could our marriage survive the difficulties that would inevitably follow in the months ahead? So many questions swirled through my head that I could hardly think about them one at a time or in any sort of meaningful order.

The drive home seemed to take forever. There was an overtaking numbness pulsing through my veins. I pulled into the driveway, climbed out, and forced myself in the direction of the front door. I stumbled up the steps and into the house where I saw Juli in the living room, laughing and having a lively conversation with my parents, who had come for a weeklong visit. I stood staring at the back of her head for a few moments, knowing that her sweet, happy spirit would in a moment dissolve away to be traded in for a world of pain and sadness. I knew that it would be a long while before I'd see her laugh again, and I wanted to savor the sounds while they lasted.

I asked her to meet me on the front porch where we sat down to talk. I told her what had happened and showed her the letter. She looked as stunned as I must have just a few hours earlier, and then in one of the most beautiful but painful moments of our marriage, she put her arms around me and said, "I'm so sorry."

"I'm the one who should be sorry," I blurted out, "but I don't even know what I've done, or not done. It just doesn't make sense."

Neither of us slept that night. The next morning we sent the kids off to school and headed to the breakfast meeting with a thousand questions between us. Who was behind this and why? What had I done to deserve this? How did this help the church in any way? Why wasn't I informed at my review if there was a problem?

Carl, the chairman of the elders, sat across from me looking bewildered as I tried to ask my questions. He finally said, "Why are you so upset?"

I gasped in angry disbelief, waving the mostly crinkled-up letter. "This makes no sense, and we don't understand,!" He asked what I was holding, and I replied, "The termination letter from you guys and Jay." With a furrowed brow he asked to see the letter and read a few lines, then turned to Barry, another elder, shook his head, and said, "This isn't at all what we talked about the other night." My anger turned into fury, and I held it all back with every ounce of strength I had. Instead of providing clarity, this meeting was only creating more confusion and causing more frustration.

Halfway through the breakfast, Jay showed up all smiles. His presence brought no more sense to our growing frustration. I wondered how all eight men, whose business successes were well-known in the community—men whose names were mentioned regularly in the local news—could have allowed their names to be attached to this mess. Though I was not too hope-filled, Carl said that the elders would meet to discuss a plan and would get back with me later in the week. No matter what the outcome of their meeting was, I had a pretty good idea that I was done. After being handled in this way, I had no confidence in anything further they might do.

I fought back anger moment by moment, but God's presence was very real. In the days that followed, a number of people were placed in my path who were obvious God-appointments. They spoke wisdom into my situation and served as a salve for the rage in my heart.

I received word that the elders had met that week each night till well past midnight trying to figure out what to do next—a sign that there was a lack of agreement about what had happened or what to do. I had little hope that much good would come out of these discussions. On Friday, the call came from Matt, another elder, requesting my presence at a Saturday morning meeting at the church. My initial response was to question why they needed me to be at the meeting since they were in the habit of making decisions that affected me without my presence. Matt said, "Listen, Doug, you never know what could happen." He repeated that, and I wondered if he was trying to communicate some coded message. Was he saying that I might keep my position and that they were going to ask Jay to leave, or was this just some trick my brain was playing on me?

Sitting at the center of the long conference table that Saturday, surrounded by Jay and the elders, I waited to hear what they had to say. Each man spoke his prearranged apology, mere sentiments void of guilt and responsibility for wrongdoing. They were sorry I'd misunderstood, sorry that I didn't agree with their actions; they were sorry I was taking it so hard. In those moments, hollow words like shells lying on a sandy beach made it crystal clear who the perpetrators were—at least one thing had finally become clear. Still, there was no retraction, and it was evident I would soon be heading in the direction of the door.

They proudly described for me three options, all which allowed me to stay on staff but only temporarily. Then the final requirement was dropped: if I chose any of these options, I would need to stand before the people in that little church, announce the plan, and tell them that it was my idea and what I wanted. To take the deal would mean I could look for another church while still holding my current position. Any ministry leader who has been in that position understands the challenge of finding a position while not holding one. I could say to any pastoral search committee that I'd decided to pursue a different ministry path, and I would be leaving my church on good terms. Every elder sitting around that table would have backed the story up. To refuse the deal would mean looking for a ministry spot with an apparent black eye. There was only one problem: this wasn't my idea, it was theirs. There was no admittance of any mistakes by the board, and everything gave the appearance that I was the one who was at fault. They clearly had no plan to take responsibility for what had happened. They held all the cards and were playing their hand carefully. In a revealing move, one of them said, "You know in business this happens all the time. You don't have to take this personally." How could I continue to work under a pastor and an elder board who would so blatantly hide the truth? How could God bless a plan forged in manipulation and dishonesty?

Though I think what I said next fell on deaf ears, I felt I had to speak to the situation from a God perspective. So I told them a story.

At the end of the book of 2 Samuel, there is an obscure and unusual story about a terrible thing David did when he was king. What did he do that was so bad? He conducted a census of his fighting men. What could be so bad about that, you may wonder. After all, shouldn't a king know what resources he has for battle? But that's just the point. The leader of God's people was to be an example of complete trust in God. Hadn't God been worthy of trust through numerous previous battles? And wasn't it God's plan to put David in this place of leadership? David should have trusted that God would continue to protect and bring victory to Israel as he had promised and as he had done.

At the end of the story, David is approached by the prophet Gad, who says that he must choose between three forms of punishment for his sin.

He could choose to have seven years of famine, to flee for three months from his enemies, or to experience three days of pestilence in the land. David responded by saying that he didn't want to fall into the hands of men but would rather fall into the hand of the Lord, and so God sent a pestilence on the land. God's leader, who in the beginning struggled to trust, had learned that it really is best to trust in God. If only he had applied that logic at the front end, how much better off he would have been!

After I finished recounting the story to the elders that day, I paused as I looked around, searching each face for some sign that my words had made a connection. The hollow reception to my thoughts left me saddened for their inability or unwillingness to connect with humility, to embrace a forthright honesty. Even after I had spoken, the looks on their faces indicated they were still waiting for my answer, so I said it plainly: "I can't accept your offer." Looks of surprise and bewilderment swept around the table, and I wondered if it was because they were genuinely concerned for my family or because they were worried about how this would appear to the church, to people I'd grown to love and respect and who loved and respected me.

There were several losers that day. My wife and family lost. The church lost, through the unwillingness of its leaders to lead—to show what it means to be humble and admit wrongs, to teach that transparency and honesty are to be sought after. The elders themselves lost. Politics and spin had trumped truth and humility, and the casualties were great.

I never did receive a solid reason for my dismissal. In hindsight, my only guess is that I'd failed to build their youth ministry fast enough. I had come from a vibrant youth program with about seventy-five students in the high school ministry and about thirty in the middle school program. Perhaps they thought that by hiring me they'd automatically have a youth ministry of the same size and scope. I had joined the staff on the heels of the discovery that several of the students in that already small youth ministry had gotten into serious trouble, and perhaps they thought that I could fix the situation. I knew that building a growing youth ministry would take some time, certainly more than eighteen months. Maybe they didn't know that.

Despite our best efforts to work with the system and build a healthy team, there will be times when we simply can't avoid conflict—and sometimes that conflict will be impossible to resolve. You may have to leave. You may get fired. Whatever the outcome, there will be times when trouble finds you. The purpose of this chapter is to give you simple ideas to get through trouble in a way that honors God and leaves you still standing at the end of the day.

Keeping Your Calling

You might be wondering why I would want to air my dirty laundry so publicly. I deliberated long and hard regarding whether or not to include this chapter of my journey here. But I know that I'm not alone, and there may be some reading this who are in deep struggle, just hanging on for one more day waiting for some hope, some glimmer of light at the other end of the tunnel. It's time for the church to rise above. It's time to quit playing politics with the bride of Christ and lay our cards on the table and say what we feel in our hearts. If we're frustrated with someone on our team, we should voice it and work it out. We're called to address our offenses with one another. The church is to be a place of honest, transparent living, and if the leaders of the church, the shotgun riders, don't stand up and be examples of transparency, then how can we ever expect the same of the church's rank-and-file? How will we ever teach it to the sheep if the shepherds aren't living it?

God has called you into his ministry. Yes, you work at a church, but your calling isn't so much to a particular congregation as much as it is to serve God himself. This calling is very personal—it's between you and him, and no one should ever be allowed to define it for you or manipulate it. It's his calling on your life, not theirs. Scripture is flush with examples of those who paid a hefty price for not honoring the call of God on their lives. Consider Jonah, who ran from his assignment; consider Abraham, who lied about his wife twice when faced with opportunities to trust that God had his back. Think of Moses, who struck the rock in anger and was kept from entering the Promised Land as a result. Consider Saul, who forfeited his kingship; and David, who paid dearly for a seemingly small act of mistrust when he conducted a census of his fighting men rather than trust in God. Don't ever be guilty of playing political games with your calling.

You are not a business partner. You're a shepherd. You were called by God, and the people sitting in those pews or in those chairs are not shareholders: they are sheep. Your calling is to tend them, to lead them, and to prepare them for works of service and train them to live righteously. It is to make disciples. And yes, sometimes you are called to shepherd even those in power.

Your people need a prophet, not a business executive. They need to be brought into connection with the truths of God's Word. And sometimes, as a shotgun rider, you may see a wolf among the sheep, and you must represent the One who called you and speak to his concerns even if it means you'll be shot off the stagecoach for it. Oh yes, you are the shotgun rider!

There are times when churches experience deep disagreement; this is a reality. Until that reality changes, I think it best to talk about it openly. To pretend it isn't so would be to ignore a certainty. Chances are good that you will find yourself in at least one extremely difficult situation in your ministry career. I find it best to go in with eyes wide open and prepared to meet the challenge face-to-face.

A wise shotgun rider will seek to rise above the mire rather than joining in it. God's messenger will avoid soiling his calling by aligning with one faction or another in a disagreement. The following thoughts come from my own experience and from what I've learned from others on the subject of church conflict. These simple ideas will help you navigate troublesome times.

RISING ABOVE THE MIRE

Several key attitudes and actions will help you when you face your own difficult situation. *First, predetermine a response when you can.* That night when I went home with the proverbial pink slip in my hand, I did the only thing I knew to do. I picked up the phone and called my friend Dan Clausen. He had served as the regional director over a five-state area for the denomination I was previously with, and since I served as the youth representative for that region, Dan and I had spent lots of time together. Dan had been involved in countless church conflict situations, and he met regularly with other experts in this field. He knew how to handle the kind of situation I was dealing with, and not in a self-preserving sort of way but in a way that could really help pastors and their churches get healthy.

His advice to me was simple. He said, "Doug, you must settle in your mind that, one way or another, you are finished at this church." He continued, "First get that solidified in your mind, and then ask God how you might help this church get healthy." He stated clearly that nothing good would come from me trying to fight to keep my job.

As much time as I had spent with Dan, this was the last thing I expected to hear him say. Truthfully, I was hoping for instructions on the proper handling of a baseball bat when knocking out someone's headlights and windshield, or at least the best way to unseat a church board! I'd told him I thought that I should get to stay and the senior pastor should have to go because of his handling of the situation, but Dan showed me how that wouldn't be good for the church. He challenged me to speak truth into the situation as I walked through it. Deep down I knew Dan was right, but I still wondered if I could do it. I wondered if I could be God's messenger to those who were handling me and my family with such carelessness.

I kept thinking, *This isn't what I signed up for*—but the truth was this *is* what I signed up for in the beginning, back when I told God that I would obey his call into ministry, to be his messenger. Sure, I signed up during a time of peace, but I was still his enlisted servant, and his message hadn't changed. Only the circumstances had changed. Sure, some circumstances are pretty important—like the one where you get a paycheck—but my being true to God's Word didn't really depend on getting paid. I realize now that a paycheck can actually get in the way of being God's messenger.

So forward I charged, the beaten-down shotgun rider with an opportunity to speak biblical truth into a difficult situation. We always jokingly say that a pastor should be ready to preach, pray, or die at a moment's notice. When you find yourself in that moment, it's time to man up—or shotgun up, as it were. The sooner you settle in with this aspect of your calling, the better off you'll be. When the time comes that you're faced with the reality of it, you'll be less likely to get squeamish.

I can't help but think about Dietrich Bonhoeffer, who left Germany in 1939 as the war was breaking out, intending to find safer haven across the ocean. Soon after he arrived in the US he was conscience stricken, feeling the need to serve with the people to whom God had called him. He headed back to Germany on the last scheduled steamer to cross the Atlantic. He was executed at Flossenburg concentration camp at dawn on April 9, 1945, just two weeks before US troops liberated the camp. The call to ministry is not a call to a paycheck or a call to comfort, it's a call to shepherd God's people and to be his messenger regardless of the cost.

Beyond your predetermination to face difficulties as God's chosen messenger, *it's necessary to seal in your mind that the church, and in particular your church, belongs to God, not you.* It's not your church; it's his. The building is his; the rooms, the tables, and the chairs are his; the budget money is his; and yes, the people are his too. Too many church turf wars could be avoided in the first place if we just lived like we really believed this.

Sometimes when I'm in a staff or board meeting and things start to get a little heated as if people are beginning to think of God's money or his church building as if it were their own, I will say, "Just for clarity, who do these funds belong to that we're discussing?" If those in the meeting seem to want to get their claws into some piece of turf or program, I'll say, "Help me be completely clear about this: For whose glory do we run this program?"

Brothers and sisters, my fellow shotgun riders, let's remind ourselves that we are shepherds, we are agents not owners, we are to be prophets not possessors. In this regard, our Catholic friends have something in their concept of the vow of poverty. Our Methodist peers, and others too, who are occasionally reassigned to a new congregation, will be more settled with the challenge of keeping themselves from digging in. They are compelled to give their lives to the church and allow the church to take care of their basic needs. Jesus told his disciples when he sent them out to take nothing with them for the journey. They were to learn to be satisfied with what he provides.

Wise shotgun riders will be clear that this world is not our home. It's all too easy to start thinking that this is my church or this is my program, and I say how it will run. "I was here when this church was started," you say. Or perhaps you even started the church yourself. Well, did you now? As I recall, Jesus said, "I will build my church" (Matthew 16:18). Are you saying that he really should have said, "You will build your church"? It's

God's church, and you merely have the privilege of being his agent.

Next, if you are to be God's agent to his church, *accept that his message will only be conveyed through love.* Don't think for a minute that politicking or manipulating your way through ministry life is going to produce spiritual fruit. Over and over again throughout your ministry, you will be dumbfounded at the means through which God shows up. Never forget that God chooses the weak things of this world to confound the wise.

And when it happens—when you see God show up and you realize it had nothing to do with your planning and scheming—stop and give him praise. Then go find a notepad and start writing it all down, and be sure to include the details of how God's work had nothing or at least very little to do with your own planning! Take note of the fact that ultimately, God doesn't need you to accomplish his will for him.

Now, back to this business of love. While God does not need you to help him out with his agenda with your cunning skill and great ministry wisdom, it's true that occasionally he will allow you to participate in some move of the Spirit, and when he does allow you to join in, it will most certainly be as a result of love. I think the Beatles and the hippies actually had one thing right: all you need is love. Love is the key. Love is the greatest pursuit, at least if you take 1 Corinthians 13:13 at face value. Nothing you do in ministry will produce spiritual results like your pursuit of love, and at no time will love be more needed or better understood than when it is least deserved.

Learn to forgive, because you'll be required to do it over and over again. I long ago gave up on waiting for my offenders to ascend to a real understanding of how they hurt me. I am no longer waiting for a statement from the church that a wrong was committed. Sometimes you just have to come to terms with it and move forward. I learned a lot about forgiveness during the eighteen months I spent out of full-time ministry following that ordeal. For example, I learned that there are really two kinds of forgiveness. There's the ideal kind, where an offending party understands at some level how they've hurt you, admits their wrongdoing, and asks for forgiveness and you, the offended party, forgive them. This is called transactional forgiveness. The second kind of forgiveness happens when there is no admittance of wrong and you, the offended person, commit before God to forgive anyway. In this kind of forgiveness the challenge is much greater, because the offense is always perceived to be greater when wrong has not been admitted.

This is the more difficult path of forgiveness, but remember that it's also the kind God is most used to offering, because we are mostly unaware of how deeply and regularly we offend him. This second variety of forgiveness takes much more work for us. All the effort falls on the shoulders of the person offended. Still it can be done, and your future effectiveness may very well depend on it.

I learned too that sometimes forgiveness is something you revisit regularly, perhaps long after the actual offense has taken place. Occasionally a name will be mentioned, and I'll think about my offenders and need to forgive them all over again. One of them drove a silver Toyota Camry, and even now, when I see a similar car driving down the road, I will feel an instant and unrequested resentment welling up within me. Again I will need to reaffirm my commitment to forgive.

I can't help but be reminded of Romans 5:8, which says, "But God demonstrates His own love for us in this: While we were still sinners, Christ died for us." While I was still a sinner, Christ died for me. I didn't and don't deserve the grace I received from Christ, and yet this is the depth of his love—and more than just the depth of his love, this is the very *nature* of it. It is the character of his love to give forgiveness when it is least deserved. It is this brand of love of which I am a recipient. And it is this very love of which I chose to be a messenger. Disagreement and conflict only provide a new avenue for that love to be given.

One of the great pearls my friend Dan shared with me in our painful phone conversation that tumultuous evening was that my offenses to God are greater than whatever wounds others have inflicted on me. Yes, I am a shotgun rider appointed to serve in the kingdom work of my holy Father, but it is when I stay close to the thought that I am an awful sinner saved only by his grace that he is best served and worshiped.

When you find yourself in conflict, look for ways to be an emissary of his love. Always speak in love. Before you ever open your mouth, ask for his love to shine through. And when you're involved in a conflict and you're pondering an appropriate response, ask Jesus to show you how to be a missionary of his grace in that situation.

Remember that the God who called you into ministry was also well aware that you'd find yourself in this situation. Perhaps he even called you *for* this situation. Sometimes it is in the foxholes and the desperate moments that God shapes and hones us for his will—to be used in greater ways. I have a theory that those who are in full-time ministry experience difficulties at a higher rate than others in the general population. I know so many ministry families with disabled children, chronic health issues, and an endless variety of other challenges. Adversity has a way of turning you toward God and developing a trust relationship that will carry you through the challenges of ministry. Perhaps it's just God's way of molding us, sharpening us, and readying us for the ride ahead.

When facing a conflict, sides are often drawn up: contemporary worship against traditional worship, fire the youth pastor or keep the youth pastor, finance the building program or don't finance it. Every church conflict has at least two sides, and each side will vie for your support. *Choose God's side.* Form a third piece in the schism, call it God's side, and begin to speak for him. Speak his truth into the situation. Ask him how you can be a light in a dark situation and then be ready to speak for him. A worthy shotgun rider will do this knowing that God promises that his Word is able to pierce into a person's soul.

Not a Detour

In the weeks and months that followed my ordeal, I came to realize that God's hand was on my life in a measure I'd never known before. The personal pains of those months was at times unbearable. I picked up whatever work a guy like me could get. I worked construction; I painted and did plaster work. I took various temporary jobs. I worked for a neighbor building decks.

At one point Juli asked me to consider leaving the ministry and finding other permanent work, and I couldn't blame her. I applied for a number of better paying jobs during that time as well, including a hotel concierge position and an office manager position. Knowing my wife was suffering because of the difficulties of ministry was torture to me. Watching her go through the pain was almost worse than the pain I was experiencing myself. And I knew she would have issues trusting that this wouldn't happen again. How could I promise her that future ministry life would be any better? It was clear we'd both been changed forever.

In spite of all the struggles, I knew what I was built for. I knew that God had called me to serve him in full-time church work, and I couldn't imagine being satisfied with anything less. I was confident he would eventually provide a way. There were times when it seemed as though God was speaking directly to me through those I met post-trauma. There was Keith, a friend from college who was ministering in a nearby town. I ran into him while taking a seminary course at his church. Keith spoke wisdom and calm into my chaotic and confused world in those first hours and days. There was a group of nonbelievers who worked with my wife and with whom we became friends. Several of those friends became seekers and eventually turned to Christ, showing us that God is at work even when he seems distant—perhaps *especially* when he seems distant.

And then there were all the ways God provided for us. We never missed one financial obligation, and still I can't explain how. I took a job at a warehouse picking orders, making less than a fourth of what the church had been paying me. The working conditions were dehumanizing, demoralizing. I felt for the people I worked with and for the way they were treated. In a way, this in itself was a ministry to my hurting heart—to know that I could bring some small sense of encouragement to everyday people. There were quotas expected of each of us that were impossible to meet without cheating the system. When you failed to meet your quota (and I often did), you were sent into the foreman's office and threatened with your job. The storeroom was housed on the second floor of a metal building with no air conditioning. The temperature in the room where we filled and wheeled our carts was at times over one hundred degrees, and any complaints about the matter were scoffed at.

Whatever little downtime I had in those hot nights at the warehouse, I spent in prayer or in making phone calls to churches that were looking for a pastor. I'd use my breaks to go out to my car and make the phone calls, and then I'd sit there and pray. I prayed that God would allow me to find a ministry position and once again have the opportunity to do what I knew I'd been called to do. I prayed that someone on some church search committee somewhere would see through the appearance that I'd done something wrong and give me an opportunity to interview with them.

I told no one at the warehouse of my situation—that is, except for Madeleine. She was a short, quiet worker, a recent immigrant from Cameroon, West Africa. Late one night I was pushing my squeaky cart, again feeling the pressure of being behind in my quota. As I rounded a corner, I nearly slammed into Madeleine's back. Looking up, I noticed that she had beads tightly braided into the cornrows in her hair, and each little bead had Jesus' name printed on it. I said, "Madeleine, your beads, do they say Jesus?" She immediately smiled back, and for the first time in about four months I heard her speak. "Yes, they say Jesus."

I ventured further, "Madeleine, are you a believer?"

She lit up with excitement; you'd have thought she had won the lottery. "Are you a believer too?" She immediately threw her arms around me, and in a thick accent she blurted out, "I'm a believer, and I've been praying to meet another Christian here. My time here is so difficult, and I have no other Christians to support me." Conscious of our quotas, we quickly got back to work, agreeing to talk later.

When the break time signal blew, I couldn't get down to the lunchroom fast enough. Madeleine was already sitting there waiting for me. I pulled up a chair at her table and there began an experience of Christian fellowship the likes of which I have rarely experienced. Each break time, we sat together and shared what God was doing in our lives and how we were trusting him with the challenges we were facing. She shared her struggle of working in less than desirable conditions while trying to work her way through medical school. Eventually I was able to tell her about my desire to get back into ministry and that God didn't seem to be answering my prayer, at least not on my timeline.

One evening, I was at the lowest point during the middle of that eighteen-month period. I had received word from two different churches that they were no longer considering me for their openings. I had no further options on the table, and I knew that once these two churches fell through, starting the process from the beginning again would mean at least another six months of praying, of hoping and waiting. As I sat down at the lunch table, Madeleine asked what was wrong. I explained the situation and said that I didn't understand what God was doing in my life. I felt that if I shared too openly the dam might burst right there in the break room. She looked squarely into my eyes and pierced my heart with one simple statement: "Doug, the will of God will never take you where the grace of God cannot keep you." That was exactly what I needed to hear. It seemed like God himself had spoken to me that evening. For the longest time I wondered if Madeleine was an angel. A couple of years later I even looked her up just to prove to myself that she was an actual person.

The dam did break, and I quickly left the room, mostly unnoticed. I headed out to the car where I buried my head and wept. These were just the words God wanted me to hear. I knew I had to become settled with the idea that I was where God wanted me, that he was in it with me, and that he would decide when and where and how I would serve him. And so, that night I began to tell God that I would trust his plan for my life, whatever it might be. My prayer times began to be less filled with anxiety and more trust oriented as I waited for God to answer my prayer. I felt a new sense of anticipation and excitement growing, not just about where he might lead me but about where he had me in that moment. Interestingly, it was about that time that everything seemed to change. I was more encouraged about my situation. Churches started taking interest in me. I felt less worry about meeting our financial responsibilities while I was unemployed, and soon after that time, I accepted a call to a pastorate—a specific and clear call that could only have been arranged by God.

As you travel along on your ride and you find yourself in difficult times, settle in with the thought that the difficulties are not a detour but rather the route chosen by God. Reject the temptation to see trials as distractions, but rather look at them as another opportunity for him to work out his plan. What looks like a detour may actually be the most direct route to the completion of God's will. The road you're taking may be for the sake of others, and even more, it may be all about preparing you for greater service in the kingdom.

Expect Dysfunction (But Don't Be Overcome by It)

Don't be surprised when you come upon dysfunction in the church. Perhaps you should even expect it; that way, when you encounter it, you won't be so surprised by it. The world is full of affliction, and the church is not immune. Neither are relationships with supervisors or team leaders exempt from the possibility of dysfunction—it's a reality of life. In any working relationship, we tend to look to our leaders for training, mentorship, and guidance. We want to know—we *need* to know—that our leaders are concerned for our growth and development. In church leadership, this need is only multiplied because of the spiritual nature of our career. The desire to be discipled and led is all wrapped up in our ambition to succeed in ministry. To divide the two is to disjoint what was never meant to be separated.

Just as in a dysfunctional family, hurt in ministry is intensified greatly when the one from whom love is needed causes pain instead. If you're experiencing this kind of pain, you will understand how challenging ministry can be because it means you work from a deficit. You may labor hard on a project or ministry hoping to please your superior and instead receive criticism, or worse, silence. You know in your head that ultimately you serve your Lord, but there's a sense in which the human touch of a leader who says "Good job" or "I appreciate your hard work" makes your work much more satisfying. Don't ever believe the lie that your desire for this kind of encouragement is unspiritual. God created each of us with human desires and emotions, and to think these emotions are unspiritual is to deny the work of our Creator.

Discipleship is ultimately a work of love: leaders love those who serve under them by developing them as leaders. Loving development and ministry leadership were never meant to be separated. When Jesus trained and prepared his followers, he didn't compartmentalize the work of ministry from his loving, discipling care over them. The two activities are meant to be intimately intertwined. John 13:34 –35 says, "A new command I give you: Love one another. As I have loved you, so you must love one another.

By this everyone will know that you are my disciples, if you love one another." Jesus's pattern of disciple making was grounded in love, and that's the way it was meant to be passed on down through the generations.

For too many leaders, the concept of growing a church has been separated from any act of love, but you cannot have the kind of kingdom growth Jesus calls us to apart from it. Can there be church growth without love? There certainly can be numerical growth, but that growth will not be the kind of discipleship Jesus taught his followers to pursue, and it's certainly not the example he left for us.

Too many church leaders expect growth to happen solely through programming decisions based on various ministry models, as if having just the right model will unlock the door to ministry growth. I have a friend who is a small group pastor at a large church. There is an expectation placed on him to have a specified and rather large percentage of attenders involved in small groups. If he fails to attain that quota, his employment will be in jeopardy. He tells me that every ministry in the church has similar expectations, with every leader given various benchmarks that define ministry success. Can you imagine Jesus strapping his disciples with these kinds of requirements? This is a way of doing ministry that does not mirror the pattern Jesus left for us. This kind of administration always leaves me wondering if the work of the Holy Spirit is bound by someone's formula or percentage.

In one of the churches in which I served, we made a refreshing effort to connect discipleship to all ministry activity. If I had a team meeting with my leaders, at the forefront of the agenda was the discipleship and development of those leaders. Once a month, all leaders of the church gathered for what we called Leadership Community, which was the centerpiece of this vision. It was a two-hour event divided into two segments. The first hour was a general session with all ministry leaders for the purpose of inspiration and vision casting. We poured ourselves into the leaders in an effort to inspire them like Jesus did with his disciples. We would regularly paint the picture for our leaders of the kind of ministry we wanted to create. The second portion was for individual breakouts with various ministries. The purpose of this segment was to equip the leaders for specific tasks and responsibilities. I would spend this time with my ministry leaders, training them and building my life into them. Much of our attention was focused on the development of leaders, and my memories are of intimate fellowship and growth.

Perhaps you've found yourself in a dysfunctional situation with your leader. If this is your lot, you will do well to review your calling. Begin by making sure of what it is God has called you to. What is the passion to which God has called you? I've found that often, your passion and God's purpose on your life are the casualties of leadership dysfunction. If you can be sure of this one thing, of God's call on your life, then everything else can be ordered in relation to it.

It's my observation that ministry dysfunction reveals three kinds of shotgun riders. First, there are those ministry leaders who are simply not capable of carrying on in the face of difficulty. If this is you, if you've tried to make it work and can't, then the best thing you can do for yourself, your calling, and your family is find a place where you *can* make it work.

Second, there are those who, when they find themselves in the midst of dysfunction, are able to carry on, not letting the neuroses around them affect their ministry. If this is you, then by all means stay. There is no reason to think that just because you are in the midst of craziness you need to get out. My friend Caleb Breakey has written a helpful book, *Called to Stay: An Uncompromising Mission to Save the Church*. It's all about staying in a church when things are not as they should be. There is help available for you if this is your situation.

There is a third type of leader who occasionally appears in these situations. This ministry leader has the spiritual understanding and disposition to confront the situation lovingly and help the church move toward health. This kind of leadership takes a person of prayer, thick skin, and keen ability to firmly apply God's truth to a messed-up church. Sometimes it means bringing in an expert third party to walk a church through a reconciliation process. If this is you, seek God for how to handle the situation you are in.

TRIALS BRING GROWTH

I recall a time shortly after I arrived at my current post when I was called on to minister to some people in crisis. Afterward, Juli asked me if I thought our detour trial a couple of years earlier had affected the way I responded. Without question, I had noticed that I possessed a new level of empathy for hurting folks and a new understanding of God's care for those in crisis. I wasn't callous or uncaring before, but there was a clear change.

You can have confidence that trials will only make you stronger. They have a way of bringing you to a better understanding of God's concern for people in crisis. They will seal in your heart that things are messed up here; they will grow in you the hope of heaven, the longing for what's on the other side. They will make you a better shepherd, a more caring leader of God's people. A wise leader knows there's no greater privilege than to be a representative of God himself, to bring light to a dark and confused world. This is the privilege and the calling of the shotgun rider.

Chapter Eight

EYE ON THE GAUGES

One weekend in college before Juli and I were married, I went to spend the weekend with her at her parents' home in the suburbs of Chicago. She met me at the door and asked me to go wait for her on the back porch, where her dad was watching television. When I—a young Bible college student—came out on the back porch, I heard the television airing the news about two well-known TV evangelists who had fallen into sin. The conversation became very awkward. Even though these two men were not from my particular variety of faith, I was ashamed. I had no good response except, "Yeah, this is bad."

Since that time, there have been numerous high-profile ministry failures—too many to count. A prideful "not me" attitude swept through our nation's church leadership, often with a condemning tone. No one ever said it, but too many of us thought it could never happen to us. You can't sweep the evidence away anymore. The personal and ministry failures of leaders in the past two decades have left in their wake scads of destroyed ministries, failed marriages, and angry kids. None of us would want that to be us, but then, I'm sure that's exactly what many of these leaders said themselves before their failures.

The experience of burnout is a serious and common problem among those who are in the ministry as well. In some ways burnout, whether we're talking about the physical or emotional variety, is as formidable an enemy as moral failure, and they often come together as a package deal—a sort of

DOUG BROWN

buy-one-get-one-free arrangement. In a 2014 poll of Christian leaders by *Leadership Journal*, it was found that less than 10 percent of leaders claimed never to have experienced burnout. That means that the other 90 percent had experienced burnout or something similar.

Burnout is something to guard against. It's a dangerous situation for several reasons. Burnout can lead to depression and stress-related physical ailments. It can deplete a leader of vitality and passion. It can also render a leader vulnerable to temptation and attacks from the evil one. Beyond all of this, burnout strips a leader of the ability to be emotionally available to those whom he or she is called to lead. Burnout can be a serious problem.

It's time to get real about it. There are just too many stories of fallen church leaders to pretend we're above it all. The failures are not just in someone else's camp anymore. We are no less vulnerable to sin than any other person—maybe more so because as leaders, we have a target on our backs, and Satan is carefully taking aim. The great question is, "How can I prevent myself from falling?"

Facing the Enemy

First in our arsenal of protection against falling has to be the recognition that we are not invincible. We must know that we too are human.

When I was growing up in church, we used to sing a song that had a couple of lines it that said, "Prone to wander, Lord, I feel it/Prone to leave the God I love." This is a characteristic of being human: we sin and we like it. I remember the first two Bible verses I memorized as a child: "The heart is deceitful above all things and beyond cure. Who can understand it?" (Jeremiah 17:9) and "We all, like sheep, have gone astray, each of us has turned to our own way; and the LORD has laid on him the iniquity of us all" (Isaiah 53:6). It's so appropriate that my childhood Bible memory program placed these two verses first out of the gate, because they are foundational to the Christian experience. None of us is above falling, and we need to guard against the spiritual pride that can take over in the mind of any Christian leader. It's easy in times of smooth ministry sailing to let down our guard and think that we are invincible, but this is the most dangerous place to be.

I was along for a ride across town with another family when we pulled

120

up to a familiar intersection frequented by homeless people, holding their cardboard signs and hoping for some handouts. I couldn't believe my ears when, from the front seat, the mom began to use the scene as a "scared straight" moment for her children. She quipped, "See what happens, children, when you make bad choices?" Where was the compassion, where was the love? She simply saw these folks as the sum of bad choices.

Sometimes we do the same thing with those who have fallen. "See what happens, Pastor, when you begin to linger at your cute secretary's desk?" Or we say, "Pity the leader who stopped taking his wife out on a weekly date." Don't get me wrong, we should all be careful to keep proper fences in place, and I'm a big proponent of the once-a-week date for *all* marriages. But if avoiding a crash-and-burn scenario is our only focus, we are shortsighted. What about the importance of day-to-day ministry vitality? What about the blessings that are missed by a halfhearted approach to ministry? If we expect God to bless our ministries, we will do well to keep our eyes on him and not on the cute secretary or any other distraction!

When it comes to matters of the heart, there is no magic formula. Our hearts are pliable and subject to being deceived. This is that truth from Jeremiah 17:9; our own hearts, which we tend to think are so pure, can actually turn against us. If we want to remain faithful, we must be on guard at a level beyond the surface; we must come to grips with the fact that we can self-deceive. I cannot offer any failsafe systems nor perfect plans, but know that there are steps that will help keep you away from sin's door and on a successful ministry path. After my almost three decades in ministry, I have learned a few things about how to keep on the right path and avoid failure. I can't really take credit for most of what I have to share, but rather I give credit to several good mentors along the way. I'm thankful that God placed some godly and right-minded leaders in my path early on who helped steer me in the right direction.

TRANSPARENCY + ACCOUNTABILITY = STRENGTH

Accountability is a good thing; it's actually a biblical concept. Proverbs 27:7 uses the picture of iron sharpening iron as an illustration of how we can sharpen each other in ministry and in living out our faith. We're told in

James 5:16 to confess our sins to each other, and in Colossians 3:16 we are taught to admonish one another.

I've always been a supporter of accountability. Every pastor and every church leader needs someone who asks the hard questions, and more than that, who will call them on the carpet when they're out of line. I feel a need, however, to herald an appeal for something more. One of my friends and ministry mentors used to say that accountability partners are great, but accountability partners can be lied to. He used to say, "If I'm going to step over the line, I'm probably just going to lie to my accountability partner about it." And it's true that if we are counting solely on someone else to keep us out of trouble, we may actually be bypassing the role of the Holy Spirit in our lives.

Yes, accountability partners are great, especially if one of the main purposes is to pray for each other's protection. More than anything, though, in the pursuit to remain pure and be set aside for Christ's service, is the great need and even greater challenge of being a person of deep character and unmovable determination. If you're going to be God's leader then God needs you to lead. The people need you to lead, and this leading must be paired with a unique transparency. Accountability is good, but it needs to be coupled with a transparent lifestyle—not so much for the sake of others but for yourself. Practicing transparent living and honesty with others at all times will demand greater character from you and bring about a more Christ-honoring life than accountability alone.

The challenge is to be brutally honest with yourself and with others. Be in the habit of bringing your junk out into the light. In doing so, you will pull the rug out from under Satan and remove any power he has in your life. When you meet with your accountability partner, don't wait for them to ask the question so you have a chance of dodging a bullet. Just charge right in and tell them about the gaps in your armor where the devil's darts have been penetrating.

I was once at a conference for youth leaders, and one afternoon I was participating in a breakout session with about fifty or so other leaders. Everyone in the room, including me, wanted to make a good impression. During one of the breaks, I got to talking in the hallway and lost track of time. Realizing that my session had already begun, I raced back into the room, interrupting the instructor. I apologized for the distraction, and without missing a beat, the wise youth leader said, "It's okay, we're just going around the room telling about our most challenging sins, and it's your turn now." For just a moment he had me, and seeing the frightened look on my face, everyone in the room enjoyed a laugh at my expense.

None of us likes having our junk exposed. I can't help but think, though, that if there was more transparency, there would be less power given over to the enemy. If we were all open about our besetting sins and temptations, they'd have a whole lot less power over us, and we'd probably have a lot more ministry victories.

I have this type of relationship with a guy on our staff. I have great trust in him, and I feel totally free to share specific sins and struggles. I find that the power this gives in ministry is freeing and life-giving. When you practice transparency, it's like emptying the chamber of the evil one's weapon.

The call of the shotgun rider hails men and women of God who are willing to rise above the tide of mediocrity and are able to persevere through the moral vacuum of this world, standing tall in God's calling on their lives. As James says, part of true religion is to keep oneself from being stained by the world (James 1:27), and if we, the leaders of the church, can't do that, then how are we ever going to expect the people in our churches to do it?

One of the senior pastors I served with used to say it was the pastor's job to stay one step ahead of the people in moral living. At the time I thought this sounded archaic and legalistic. Now, much later, I understand what he was saying in a different light. The system of the world is set against us, and no one is more targeted by the evil one than those at the front line. Our moral standards need more vigilance to uphold than the average Christian's.

THE POWER OF LONG-TERM THINKING

Our world has become so sexualized and set against our Christian values that it's more of a challenge to be set apart than ever before. I'm beginning to think that our Amish friends have something as I find myself on guard more and more as time passes. I find myself watching less TV and spending less unplanned time on the computer than I once did. Any shotgun rider who is committed to long-term success in the ministry will want to get used to the challenge of remaining pure.

We used to have some pretty cool discussions in my church youth group when I was a kid. We loved to get into debates with our youth leaders in an effort to stump them. One thing I remember is how we used to ask them if certain activities were okay. Most of these questions had to do with the opposite sex. For instance, we wanted to know, was it okay to kiss a girl on the first date, or was it okay to be alone together in a dark room? The big muse was the question, "How far is too far?" What I know now is that we were asking the wrong questions. The right question might have been, "How can I stay as far away from falling as possible?" Fewer of us ask that question. We don't like that one because we perceive that it will suck the fun out of our existence.

In reality, the opposite is true. Scripture says in Proverbs 6:27, "Can a man scoop fire into his lap without his clothes being burned?" Anyone who has ever had a small child in the kitchen when they were cooking knows the scene. We say, "Don't touch that, you'll get burned." And what's the first thing they do? They touch it. In reality, this is not a phenomenon of childhood as much as it is a phenomenon of personhood. Entering the ministry with a plan for longevity will greatly enhance our ability to stay clear of trouble. We must begin by training ourselves to ask the right questions. Character and reputation is everything in ministry, and we build it one week, one day, and one interaction at a time. The sum total won't be measured until the end. Have a plan, and not just for the immediate future; look to build career-long thinking that will meet us on the other end and welcome us with open arms.

GAUGE WATCHING

We were well on our way to our Christmas destination—visiting my family in Oklahoma for the holidays—when the trouble began. I first noticed a hissing sound coming from under the car as we left the restaurant at our midway stop. I became concerned as we loaded up the kids for the second leg of our journey, so I got down under each tire. I couldn't find any signs of a leaky tire, so I wrote it off as coming from another car next to ours, and off we went. About two hours later, a warning light came on at the dash warning that the car was overheating. We took the first exit, but I feared it was too late as the car started shaking and vibrating. I could smell burning metal. We discovered later that the hissing sound I'd heard back at the restaurant was a tiny hole in a radiator hose, and over the last couple of hours, all the coolant had leaked out. That little pinhole cost us an engine rebuild, a new transmission, and a whole lot of stress in our holiday experience.

There's something to be said for keeping your eye on the gauges, not just in our cars but in our lives as well. Certain signs tell us when we're getting into dangerous territory, things that alert us about what else is going on in our bodies and in our souls.

Sleep is a great indicator of our overall health. When we're not sleeping well it's good to find out why. I once went in for one of those sleep studies, where they hooked me up to all kinds of wires and sensors. (It's my conclusion that the term "sleep study" is an oxymoron, because the technicians are constantly coming into the room and waking you up, and there's not much sleep that actually happens.) In the morning I asked what they had learned, and the nurse said they couldn't determine anything because I never actually slept. That was really encouraging, so I probed further, and she said the test showed I had clenched or ground my teeth over eight hundred times in a four-hour period. She then asked what I was stressed about. Jokingly, I told that I was stressed about not sleeping—but as it turns out, that's just what I discovered over the next few weeks. Through the help of some good friends and a wise doctor, I learned that I was actually stressed about being stressed. Weight gain, headaches, irritability, depression, and yes, sleep are all like those pesky lights on our dashboard, and it's generally a good idea not to ignore them.

One of the most important gauges to keep our eye on is time with our heavenly Father. Every believer needs this connection with the Father, and keeping it up is an indicator of overall spiritual health. When I used to teach this to my youth, they would always ask me if it was better to spend time in the morning or in the evening, and was it okay if they only hit three out of five days each week? These are great questions, and the fact that they were even asking was a positive sign. One of the most important things we do to maintain our spiritual health is to spend time with our Father. We talk about spending time in the Word, but let's be real, not all the time we spend in the Word is actually time spent with the Father. As ministers, we spend so much time preparing for Bible studies and devotionals and teaching times that we are often more like college kids cramming for a test than we'd like to admit. Don't get me wrong, it's really important that we be students of the Word, but knowing about the Bible, or even teaching it, isn't the same as knowing its Author.

I'm motivated by the times that Jesus spent with his Father. Scripture says, "But Jesus often withdrew to lonely places and prayed" (Luke 5:16). Here's the Savior of the world in need of intimate time with his Father, and it says he did this often. We should take the same attitude. When I'm asked questions like those my youth group students asked, I like to respond by turning it around and teaching that we should spend as much time with the Father as we need. Generally, we know when we're not spending enough time with God.

When I was a teen and developing in my own spiritual walk, I recall times when I felt a general frustration and anger toward the world. My attentive mother would notice and ask if I'd been spending time in the Word. She would suggest that if I spent time with God, he would help me adjust my attitude. A wise follower will pay attention to this gauge and be sure to spend time with the Father. Our gauges generally tell us when we're depleted and need to fill our tank, so let's pay attention!

Anger is another of those danger signs. One of the most helpful things I've ever read about anger is found in James 1:20, and it says that "Human anger does not produce the righteousness that God desires." God doesn't need our anger! It actually gets in the way of him accomplishing his work through us. Sometimes we get angry while trying to make a project go through, or we try to deal with someone who has blocked our plans by using our anger to plow over them. Be sure this is one way to get things done, but whatever gets done won't be in line with God's purposes, at least according to James.

It's a good idea to get a handle on anger early in your ministry, before unhealthy patterns set in. What are the things that really make you angry? Although we—not outside factors—are ultimately responsible for our anger, it's good to know what it is that triggers our anger so we can learn to handle it appropriately. Somehow we have to learn how to take those anger-producing circumstances and turn them into positive change.

One way to get on top of your anger is to make a pact with yourself never to have conversations when you're angry. Also, it's a good idea to leave as much work at the office as possible. Don't take your anger home and dump it on your wife and kids. I'll admit this is very difficult—we too often carry the pain of ministry around with us, and it's a challenge to keep our family from absorbing it.

It's a good idea to find a trusted ministry friend and make an agreement that you will discuss the things that make you angry, pray about them, and get another perspective. We all need a prayer partner! I have built this kind of relationship with a couple of friends in ministry. Occasionally, when I find myself smoldering about something I will ask for their perspective, and they have done the same with me. We call this talking each other down from the ledge. In the process, I've learned that often, the things I'm fired up about turn out to be nothing at all. Having someone to bounce your emotions off of helps you carve out a godly and productive plan for action as opposed to giving way to destructive reactions.

It sounds silly, but *regular exercise curbs negative emotions and helps us avoid downward spirals.* I don't know if it's the endorphins or just the increased oxygen, but I find that when my exercise routine is regular, I'm able to handle stress more effectively, and I generally feel healthier.

Keep a check on your pride. One bright and sunny Sunday afternoon, my three children and I were driving home from church. A mile down the road, we eased up to a stoplight, and in the car next to us a rather hardened-looking man was enjoying a cigarette. The smoke gently drifted our way in the warm spring air, and he appeared to be savoring every puff. My daughter, barely old enough to be sitting in the front seat, was riding shotgun. Apparently feeling all of the command her front-seat position was due, she glanced over at the man and cut through the smoke and the short distance between us with one accusing word: "Smoker!"

I'm sure the guy heard my wordless gasp, and I only hope he didn't know us from church! After what seemed like forever, the light turned green, and as we pulled away, the heat slowly faded from my face and there began a discussion in our car—the teaching portion of that teachable moment. We talked about our responses to those we meet; we talked about people who were struggling to quit smoking, people we knew. I wanted to cut through the judgment and put a human face behind the cigarette. We can all use more of that perspective. I learned that our school system had done a good job instilling the dangers of smoking in my daughter the week before, perhaps a little too good. But she provided a mirror for me at that moment: sometimes as we're riding shotgun, we become anesthetized to our own pride.

Pride is one of the perils of the shotgun ride. Pride is dangerous. When you're infected with it, those who rub shoulders with you can smell it a mile off. They'll often recognize it's a problem long before you even know it's there. Pride is the opposite of humility. Like a light breeze on a candle, it will snuff out humility. Pride hoards credit, while humility shares it with others. Pride cloaks God's work, while humility opens the way for him to shine. Pride is a consumer of oxygen, while humility is life-giving. And most of all, pride stands in direct opposition to grace. Grace is about what God did for us, not about what superior qualities we have to offer. Pride says I did it, and grace says *he* did it—more than that, he did the doing while we were still wallowing in our sin.

Pride is not just a struggle for leaders at the top. Even in the shotgun seat, pride can be a problem. However, when you truly realize the implications of your call to ministry, there is no room for pride. Everything about being in the ministry should stand in direct opposition to pride as our central message is grace. To begin with, the spiritual gifts that were given to us to serve didn't come from our own effort. God gave them to us so we could serve him. Likewise, our calling came from God, not from our own initiative. At core, our entire faith is based on our need for something outside of ourselves. Even our salvation is a gift from God that was neither earned nor deserved. And if for a moment we think the results we see in our ministry are somehow related to our own strength and effort, then we've just proven that pride is getting in the way of God using us in ministry.

I weary at times from ministry model fatigue. Discussions about church models always seem too man-centered. So many "successful" churches promote one ministry model or another. I have sat at these tables where the great ministry models are being discussed and analyzed, yet Scripture tells us that God is directing the affairs of men. We know that Jesus said he would build his church, so what credit can we take if God chooses to use a particular model in one church or city and a different model in another locale? Who are we to take credit for what God does? And if success is a result of our great ministry model, then what do we need God for? To bless our ministry model, of course, because I'm sure that God is just waiting around for a brilliant enough mind to come along and create a model worthy of his blessing. Because he needs us like that...or so we think.

Take a good inventory of your character and extinguish pride if you find it. Do it now before it gives birth to grief, for yourself and for those around you. Dispel any notion that you are the great architect of any of your successes in ministry, and realize that every good and perfect gift comes from above (James 1:17).

Every shotgun rider will want to keep an eye on the gauges, not only to keep from major moral failure or burnout but to build a ministry that has a foundation of personal moral purity. Day-to-day ministry vitality depends on it.

CHAPTER NINE
GUIDING PRINCIPLES

You have them whether you know it or not—we all do. We all have a set of operating principles. They may be well thought-out, or you may not even to be able to verbalize them. Either way, they are what drive you. They determine how you think, and to a large degree, they are good predictors of how you will respond in many ministry situations.

We generally think of our operating principles as always being spiritually motivated—and ideally they always would be—but often they can be things we learned growing up or even through the conditioning of our culture. Wherever they come from and however you acquired them, you have them and they are ultimately what shape your ministry.

That being true, it's important for us to intentionally examine and shape our guiding principles. I've found that many of us aren't able to put into words the things that determine our direction in ministry; we just go about our business doing what we do without ever questioning why. It's wise to write down what you think are the principles that are behind your actions. This will help you both with verbalizing for others what you feel is important to your calling and with fixing things that need to be corrected.

The following are my own operating principles. Feel free to learn from my experience as you need and chuck what you feel is irrelevant. The point is not so much that you adhere to my particular principles (although I'm convinced they can help you survive and even thrive). It's more important that you are able to verbalize your own. I've spent quite a bit of time over the years studying how our beliefs and values affect our ministry, and my experience tells me that our guiding principles determine how we respond and act in every ministry situation.

PRINCIPLE 1: GRACE IS EVERYTHING

Everything in the Christian life comes down to grace. More than anything else, this is what steers me in ministry, and it's what directs me in my private life too.

As ministers of the gospel, we define for others what it means to be Christ followers. All too often, that definition comes in the form of lists which get passed along from generation to generation and become our picture of what it means to be "Christian." We subtly teach others that if they want to be Christians, they must do these things on our lists, and we teach them to avoid certain other things, because this is what Christians do or don't do. Yet much of what we blindly pass along has little to do with Christianity.

Why is it that we continue to paint a picture of our faith that might not be very Christian at all? It's not that these things on our lists aren't good; it's just that they sometimes aren't particularly Christian, and further, if parishioners are going out to face the world with nothing more than a list in their pocket, what have we really given them?

Interestingly, popular notions of what is considered "Christian" differ from culture to culture. In some parts of the world, Christians take their shoes off when they enter a church building. Not to do so would be a great offense. In some other places, it is considered un-Christian for a woman to wear shorts. There was a time in our own culture when it was thought of as un-Christian to dance or play cards or even enter a movie theater. In a particular Latin culture with which I am familiar, the pastors of churches are deeply involved in the marriage decisions of young couples who are courting. To move ahead toward marriage without the pastors' blessing just doesn't happen. This is where grace comes in. If we had to define Christianity in one word, what would that word be? If we had to reduce it all down to one concept that would define all Christians in every culture and place and time, what would that concept be? It would be grace. That's what we were given when we became a Christian. We received grace, accepting it as a gift from a holy God, the one thing we could neither earn nor purchase: the forgiveness of our offenses against him.

Why is it, then, that so much of what we continue to pass along from generation to generation is altogether different from grace? These lists and definitions are poor substitutes for the grace we received when we placed our faith in Christ. While they might create the shell or appearance of good Christian character, they are poor reflections of our grace.

So many things within Christendom get promoted as the important matter. Various movements have dominated Christianity through the ages, emphasizing different aspects of our faith. There have been prayer movements of various kinds. There have been movements to take Christianity back to the city and others to take Christianity out into the country. There have been various methods of childrearing, complete with guides for discipline and the promise that your kids will turn out right. There have been numerous man-motivated revival movements and waves of prophetic conferences. In recent years we have heard much about the seeker movement and what it means to be seeker-friendly, seeker-sensitive, or seeker-aware. Even more recently, there has been a health and wellness emphasis in the Christian media.

All of these are good, but sometimes when you talk to those who have sold out to any one of these micromovements or persuasions, you might begin to wonder how Christianity has survived these two thousand years without their particular emphasis. Our current situation is not exempt. I've often wondered: If I fail to mention in my Twitter bio that I'm concerned about social justice or human trafficking because I've dedicated that space to mentioning my work with orphans, can I still be considered valid? Movements continue to come and go. The only emphasis that has survived the history of Christianity is grace, and that is because it is the very essence of our faith.

The message of God's grace is even transferable cross-culturally, and every Christian in every era is a recipient. I love to hear others tell the story of how they came to Christ. I've heard the stories from people from all over the world, people from many countries and from various economic and cultural backgrounds, and every time I hear variations of the same thing. I hear someone say, "I was lost, and I came to realize that I needed Jesus's cleansing forgiveness, so I repented of my sin—and though I did nothing to deserve it, Jesus forgave me and gave me new life." Every believer should understand this grace, because it is the door through which each entered the faith.

No matter who we were or how sinful we were before we met Jesus, we all came humbly to Christ and dipped from that same pool of his grace. This is the one thing that characterizes Christians of all cultures and through all generations. Grace is the important thing; it's our one sustainable resource in the Christian faith.

Most of us who lived through the post 9/11 years are at least somewhat familiar with the capture, trial, and execution of Saddam Hussein. What most people aren't as familiar with is how this tyrant came to power in the first place. Early on, he had worked his way up through the ranks to become the leader of the Baath party and later prime minister. In these roles he gained power and control over the government little by little. In 1979 he forced the president, who was his cousin, out of office.

After taking control, his first order of business was to call a meeting of the top party officials, at which he directed one of the members to read a confession of disloyalty to the party. The confession was brokered with a promise of immunity if the man would also give up the names of others who were disloyal. As the names of sixty-eight party leaders were read, one by one these well-dressed and highly educated men stood and were escorted out of the assembly. Days later in a trial that lasted less than two minutes, twenty-two of these men were sentenced to death and executed by men selected from among those whose names were not called. The rest received long-term prison sentences, and the man who was promised immunity was among those executed.

Saddam had the whole event recorded, then distributed throughout the country to create a sense of fear. In the video you can see well-dressed men weeping in fear that their names would be called. Some tried to defend their honor and innocence but were silenced and helplessly escorted out of the room. In fits of panic, some men can be seen shouting their declarations of loyalty and allegiance to their new leader. All this happened while Saddam sat calmly puffing on a cigar and smiling.

This kind of leadership was characteristic throughout his reign. His presidency was always carried out by brute force. In the initial days of his rule, some four hundred men of his own party were executed for various stated reasons. The public face of Saddam was grandfather-like, but behind the scenes he ruled with brutality, fear, and terror. Using chemical weapons, he tried to eliminate the Kurdish people, and in one chemical bombing raid alone a village of five thousand people was wiped out. His message was clear: follow or die.

What I take from this is that the characteristics of Saddam's reign were set in motion by the way it began. So it is for the gospel—a message that could not contrast more with the brutality of a regime like Saddam Hussein's! Grace itself characterizes the way we pass it on. At the core of the Christian message is the fact that a holy God sent his one and only Son to earth to live and die for us so that the penalty of our sin could be met. At the very heart of the matter, this grace is an undeserved, unearned gift, and this has huge implications for the way it is shared and also in the way our faith is lived out every day.

Grace means that we must love others the way Jesus loves us. The gospel message is not spread through force or through manipulation, but through love and self-sacrifice. Christ laid out this example in dying for us.

Grace requires that we respect others. As Christian leaders, we must treat our brothers and sisters in Christ as fellow travelers, not as pawns to be manipulated or used. In recruiting, for example, I always explain what the task or ministry position is and ask the person to think and pray about it for a week or so. I always assure them that the decision is really between them and God and that I won't ever twist their arm or harangue them.

At the core of grace is the idea that we've been forgiven of much, and because we've been forgiven, we must be forgiving toward others. This is the point of Jesus's story about the man who was forgiven a great debt and went out to beat a servant who owed him a very small debt. Those who understand grace will be more likely to share it with others.

Grace demands that we trust others. This is often an overlooked idea in ministry. Too many ministry leaders carry with them a mistrust of their volunteer leaders or staff. We communicate this mistrust in many ways; for instance, if we are constantly checking up on those whom we lead, it says that we don't trust them. I once heard a Christian speaker say, "People don't do what you expect; they do what you inspect." At the core, this kind of leadership is not in the spirit of grace. A leader who constantly reminds his people of tasks and assignments shows that he doesn't really believe they will follow through. A leader who is autocratic with authority communicates that he or she doesn't trust volunteers or directors to think or act on their own. Ultimately, we must trust that God will lead in others' lives just as he leads in ours. Trusting our team members shows that we trust God.

Ultimately, mistrust of others on our team is a mistrust of God. If we really believe that God gives gifts, talents, and creative abilities to others, then we should trust him to use those people for his service. After all, doesn't the Scripture say that he who began a good work in the lives of his followers will complete it (Philippians 1:16)? A good leader knows how to encourage his or her people, allowing their God-given talents and abilities to flourish.

Grace also means that we don't give up on others, no matter how far from God they seem. Remember that love hopes all things (1 Corinthians 13:7). It's been my observation that it's often those who seem farthest from God who end up turning to Christ. Through the years I've kept prayer lists of people who need Christ. On these lists there would be both religious and irreligious friends. There would be those I would consider friendly to the gospel and those I would say are clearly unfriendly to it. Some of those on my lists have now become believers, and while the last chapter is obviously still to be written, so far those seemingly farthest from God are leading those who seem close by about two to one. It seems our God delights in drawing those who would mock him and resist his call.

Grace also demands that we don't trust in the power of men but in the strength of God. Remember that God confounds the wise by using the weak. The popular church leadership notion today is that if we fill our staffs with high performers, we will find greater success. Just read through some ministry job ads, and you'll get the idea. Some of these descriptions use terms like "fast-paced," "high-energy," and "able to build dynamic, high-performing teams." No doubt high performers produce results, but I can't help but wonder: if the results we're looking for require a peak performer, then why does God need to show up? Remember the appointment of David as king over Israel? He wasn't exactly the front runner for that important political position, was he? It seems backwards to us, but God's ways are not man's ways.

"The student is not above the teacher, but everyone who is fully trained will be like their teacher" (Luke 6:40). This has always been a challenging verse for me to get my head around. It says that when our students are fully taught, they will be like us, their teachers. One way or another, most of those who come into our ministry will eventually leave. Students graduate and move on, and the older folks in our congregations get transferred out for one reason or another. The great question is, what will they take with them when they leave?

I hope my students and ministry partners, those who are under my tin roof, take with them a love for Jesus. I've had this desire for my own children as well. What I mean by this is not the stereotypical Jesus-love pictured for us by the media, and certainly not the hollow Jesus-love that is sometimes familiar in our Christian circles, like the one who waves a Christian flag in your face and commands personal attention with his own charismatic personality. I am not talking about a man-made, hyped-up caricature of Jesus-love. No, I want my kids and those I have discipled to be a different kind of Jesus-lover. I want those within my influence to have an authentic love for Jesus, not a proud, overconfident, self-determined love, but a responsive, respect-filled, thoughtful love. When they are observed by others, I would like to think they will be noted as distinctively Christian, not because of a bumper sticker or a fish on their car, not because of a cleverly worded T-shirt or a cross around their neck, and not because of a busy weekly schedule of church involvement, but because of the way they interact with others in genuine concerned love—love that in the first place, they received from Jesus.

I want them to have a deep understanding of who Jesus is and what he has done for them. If they know him and experience him, I'm confident they will love him, and because of knowing him deeply and therefore loving him, they will be different on the inside, where it really matters. I want them to have something within that will drive them, motivate them, and direct their actions and their attitudes about others. After all, Jesus himself said these are the two greatest commandments to live by: to love God and to love others. *I want those I lead to love others as Jesus did and does, and that means they must get grace; it must be infused into their very being.* Sure, I could use coercive means to get others to be loving or forgiving. It is possible to produce the results, the outcomes you want through manipulation, but the gospel of grace is meant to be lived from the heart, and that means it must first take root in the heart.

We are all passing on something. We must ask ourselves what it is that we're passing on if it isn't grace.

For this reason, grace should steer every activity in ministry. When I mull over that truth, I think of an epic story. In my estimation, it is the greatest story of our era. Fifty years in the making, it has spawned one major motion picture, many documentaries, and even a children's cartoon version of the story. The events were first made famous in the 1956 January 30 issue of *LIFE* magazine, and they have been written about in *Time* and other major publications as well. It is the story of the Waodani Indians and the way God's grace was brought to them by a group of missionaries whose names are still well-known to many of us: the Elliots, the Saints, and others.

It isn't often that the world pays much attention to the work of Christian missionaries. So why was there so much interest in this real-life drama as it unfolded? Like stories of miners trapped below the earth or space capsules in perilous danger in outer space, this event has captivated us. From the very beginning, when five young missionary men were speared to death on a river beach in the jungles of Ecuador, the world has watched. This story has deeply affected many, and because of it, thousands have given their lives to serve Christ around the globe. As the world looked on, it contemplated the events in disbelief and debated a proper response, and all the while the several missionary families continued to bring the gospel of grace to the very ones who did the killing.

I have been gripped by this story myself, and I have often wondered how those missionary families could go right back into the jungle and work with those who killed their husbands and fathers and brothers. The answer is both easy and difficult at the same time. The easy answer is that the gospel wouldn't be the gospel if it was only given to those who deserved it. If it had to be earned, it wouldn't be the gospel of grace. But that answer is difficult because sometimes there is a great cost in the delivery of grace. Sometimes the cost lasts a lifetime, and yes, sometimes the cost is one's very life.

Maybe the reason this story has captured the world in such a powerful way is not simply because five well-intentioned, innocent men lost their lives in a dangerous foreign jungle, but because it is exactly the story the world needs and is looking for. Maybe the world needs this kind of grace, and maybe, just maybe, people in the world are more self-aware of the human situation than we realize.

The world needs more missionaries like you and me, willing to pass on the grace we've been given. The families that went back into the jungle to live among that tribe have given us a contemporary example of what a normal Christian life should be. The fact that they did this difficult task with joy and love is both a catalyst for the media attention they attracted and a challenge to all of us. They've shown us that it is our joyful privilege to pass along what we have been given. They have taught us that passing on grace to others is the normal Christian life.

It's my conviction that this grace shapes everything in ministry. When one of your ministry volunteers reveals an impending divorce, you may indeed need to find a replacement, but more importantly, you will have a ministry of grace in their life as well. And when someone lashes out at you and you know there's some other reason for the anger you've received, this too is an opportunity to offer grace and teach it with your life.

The first pastor I served under had been a pastor for thirty-two years in the same church, and he had seen a lot of stuff over the years. He used to say "Wounded dogs bite," pointing out that often when people are in pain, they lash out at those around them, even those who are trying to offer help to them, those who are called to serve them. Don't look at that person as your enemy, but see them as someone who needs a grace response.

When the parent of one of the students you work with complains about your ministry, you have an opportunity to live out grace. Too many times we make things personal that don't really need to be. A mature leader is one who knows how to turn these situations into a positive experience.

And without question, your ministry with those outside the body of Christ will have a grace aspect. In fact, it's all about grace, isn't it? We have what the world needs. We have been gifted with the greatest gift one could ever be given, and there are those all around us who need what we have. We have Jesus, and the world needs Jesus. We've been given grace, and they need grace. Grace is everything.

Principle 2: Shepherd First

One of the neat things in the Spanish language is its relationship to the word *pastor*. The word is spelled the same in both English and Spanish, but in Spanish, the word for *pastor* is the same as the one for *shepherd*. So when introducing a pastor, you would say, "Meet my friend, Doug. He's the shepherd of families." I love that because the term so clearly describes our biblical responsibility—in fact, our English word *pastor* also comes from a Latin root meaning shepherd or herdsman. We are to be the shepherds of God's flock.

Before anything else I'm a pastor, a shepherd. That means my first priority is to shepherd people. Perhaps in today's church culture, the word *shepherding* seems out of place. It's true that we don't use the term much anymore, but it's ultimately what we are all to be about in the church. So what does it mean to shepherd?

The essence of my calling is wrapped up in being a pastor. If you've been given the spiritual gifts of pastor/teacher, if God has placed in your heart a desire to pastor, then your primary calling is all about shepherding. I would even go one step further and say that all those who work in a church in one capacity or another should be about shepherding. Even if your position isn't about shepherding in some clear way, you are probably still involved in the task of shepherding, and no matter what your job title is, you can still be a shepherd to those you serve.

You say, "Well, I was only hired to work at the reception desk." Or perhaps you were hired to do administrative work for the worship pastor. At core, every church's number-one assignment is the Great Commission. We are to go and preach the gospel by teaching and baptizing, so the pastor of the church—I mean the big pastor—is supposed to lead the charge in completing this assignment. It only follows that all those who work on his team are to assist him with this task. For a church to be doing something other than the Great Commission is to be something other than what God has designed his church to do. So all of us, no matter what our job entails, should have the shepherding of people in view. In that sense, we are all ultimately pastors. We are to lead people first and foremost.

When I was a youth pastor, people used to tell me how impressed they were with the way I was able to relate to young people. I always responded that God had placed within me the desire and calling to shepherd—it just happened that I was able to relate to teens, so that was where I was shepherding. In more recent years in my work with children and their families, I would hear similar comments, and my reply was the same: "I'm a pastor first and foremost, it just happens that I'm currently a pastor to families."

Perhaps you are one of the many staff members today without "Pastor" or "Reverend" in front of your name, yet whatever your title, ultimately the bulk of your focus is going to be pastoral in nature. Yes, there are many people who are employed by churches who have task-oriented responsibilities. No matter what our specific work in the church is, somehow it should aid in making disciples and shepherding saints.

If you're at the beginning and just starting to explore the possibility of a life in the ministry, if you feel God tugging you toward a ministry path, then it would be wise to begin to think pastorally. That is, learn how to make disciples and shepherd people. If you think that you might want to climb that ministry career ladder, so to speak, then remember that whatever is further up that ladder is only going to be progressively more pastoral and involve more shepherding and disciple-making.

There is a misconception that you can be a great leader in the church and somehow bypass the need to take on shepherding responsibilities. Some young leaders dream that their speaking abilities or great organizational skills will someday put them before a large congregation. It is true that there are a few great speakers/pastors out there who could walk into any town and within a matter of weeks build a large following based on their dynamic speaking abilities, their superior relational abilities, or their great name. Let's be real, it happens. The truth is, though, that you generally don't keep people around if you're not actually leading them. History shows that no great church is ever sustained whose leaders don't care about people, about souls.

When I came to the church where I now serve, there was a great discussion about what the children should call me. Everyone wanted to weigh in on the matter. When I caught wind of the discussion, I quickly made my preference known. I wanted them to call me Pastor Doug. Not because there is some great respect that comes with that particular title, but because I wanted them to know that this was the role I wanted to play in their lives. To this day, many of those children, though grown, still call me Pastor Doug, and I still have that same role in their lives.

Whether or not you wear the title "pastor," if you are in ministry, be sure that you are to be a shepherd to the people to whom God has called you, starting with those who are under your tin roof. In my title and in my interaction with others, my role will always be to shepherd God's people.

Principle 3: People before Programs

One of the greatest struggles for the shotgun rider comes in the area of programs. Most of our job descriptions are laden with programs that are our responsibility to run and maintain. In my current position, I'm responsible to oversee our church's midweek children's program, our two Sunday morning children's programs, a summer camp, our summer midweek Super Ten Club for kids, and Vacation Bible School. I also oversee several leaders, including a director who runs an on-site preschool, an early childhood director who runs all of our preschool children's care and programs, and our women's ministry director, who hosts several programs each year. I also direct a team responsible for a large yearly marriage-and-parenting conference.

All that to say, I write as someone who is quite familiar with programs! I understand what is involved in planning and carrying them out. I get the importance of schedules and team meetings and delegation. The truth is, though, that I also understand that programs are not the most important thing. People are. Programs are only a means to meet the spiritual needs of people. So if you find yourself swallowed up by too much program responsibility, it's time to make a change—a change in your ministry or a change of your ministry location if necessary. Keeping people the main focus is the central priority, and it's that important.

The challenge is to make program plans simple enough so as not to get in the way of your ability to connect with people. We have great ways of taking plans that could be simple and making them complicated. Programs in general have a way of taking on a life of their own, and they can become a weight around your neck. In team meetings, I find myself constantly looking for ways to make programs less complicated and involved. All this is so that I can spend less time keeping the proverbial plates spinning and spend more time with people.

If you find yourself with a program that has died, feel free to bury it, at least for a time. Our church had a program for young mothers for a number of years. For most of two decades, the ministry was strong and well-staffed. Over time it became more and more challenging to find leaders who were passionate about running it. I made the decision to end the ministry. When I came to the church where I now serve, there had been a large puppet ministry involving a dozen or so volunteers. Several people indicated that they were glad I had come on staff because they were waiting for me to take over the ministry. I learned, however, that all of the volunteers had quit and were not interested in continuing. It would have been foolish for me to try to continue something that was already dead. I would have had a coronary trying to work all of those puppets on my own.

People always come before programs, and no program is worth running just for its own sake.

Principle 4: Leaders Lead

One of the greatest mistakes of shotgun riders is to assume that all leadership belongs to the senior pastor. Those who are in associate- or director -level roles often allow themselves to believe that they do not need to lead because it's really someone else's job. When leadership questions come up, there is a tendency to defer to the senior pastor or some other person up the chain. This is certainly an easier route, but it is a cop-out that only foments a leadership vacuum.

People want to be led; they need to be led. People need leadership. "Where there is no vision [leadership] the people are unrestrained" (Proverbs 29:18, NASB). Sometimes I've heard pastors say, "Nothing gets the saints excited like the smell of wet cement." Any forward movement gets people excited, and to some degree it also draws giving. It is said that you can't steer a parked car. People want to be led, and churches that lead tend to draw followers. I have known of churches that have undergone unusual projects that seemed so unconventional that I questioned their practicality, yet people were drawn because they saw movement.

For a short time a few years back, my family and I attended Northpoint Community Church, pastored by Andy Stanley outside of Atlanta. During the time we were there, the church was struggling through growing pains. They had already begun a couple of satellite campuses and were bursting at the seams on their main campus. I remember hearing one Sunday about their plan to expand, and at first I thought I must have misunderstood what they were saying. The plan was to build an additional auditorium space directly behind the existing one. The new space would face opposite the existing one, so this was not simply an enlarging of the existing room. The plan allowed for there to be concurrent services with multiple worship teams leading simultaneously in the two spaces. The pastor could speak from either auditorium and be broadcast into the other space via video feed.

At first I thought it was the craziest thing I'd ever heard. Why not just enlarge the existing space to allow for greater attendance in the same room without the crazy configuration? But the plan was even more unusual than that: when the project was completed, attenders were asked to sit in alternating auditoriums based on their last names. Every week you were to sit in a different auditorium so that every other Sunday you could experience the message live. Whatever Northpoint's motivations were for the unusual plan, I can tell you that the response of the attenders was welcoming—even overwhelming. People are attracted to forward-thinking leadership even when their plans are unconventional.

Of course, good leadership doesn't always have to involve a construction project. People aren't necessarily looking for a church with physical growth, just growth. My Canadian college roommate always used to say, "Leaders lead." He would usually invoke this quote when I was hesitant about asking a particular girl out or when he was trying to lure me into some crazy scheme he was cooking up, but I've come to own the principle because it's true: leaders do lead.

You can understand my roommate's statement in two ways. First, much of leadership is tied up in initiative. So if you're going to be a leader, you will need to show initiative. If you want to be a leader, lead! Second, leaders are the ones who are leading. That is, if you want to know whether someone is a leader, look to see if anyone is following him or her. Too many so-called leaders are posers who talk like leaders, associate with other leaders, and can quote great leaders, but in reality they have no followers and are simply not leading. Too many leaders look to see where the people are headed, then jump in front. This is not leadership; it's actually more like following.

Good leadership is rare, and when it is lacking or even absent in the church, people get frustrated and look for it in other places. Churches with weak leadership are always in danger. They are in danger of doctrinal error, in danger of disintegrating, and most of all, in danger of losing their effectiveness. In even the worst of leadership situations, however, the shotgun riders can fill a vacuum and help a church survive, and yes, even thrive. How does this work out practically? How does a lower-level associate provide leadership when they're not at the helm? I'm not talking about the kind of leadership that sets the vision and direction for the church, for which you might need to be in a senior position. I contend that leadership is unrelated to position and can be offered from any place.

There are several ways you can lead when you're not the leader: First, to a certain degree, your leadership must be consistent with the stated direction the church is already heading. Even though your church's leadership might be weak, you must be headed in the same direction or you will only provide further frustration. Those who lead people away from the direction the church is headed aren't leading but simply causing dissension.

Second, all good leadership begins with relationships. You cannot effectively lead people you don't know or care about. People will follow someone through pretty crazy plans if there is a relationship built on trust.

When I was in grade school, there was a skating pond on my way to school. In the summer it was a place to jump your dirt bike, and in the winter it was a skating rink. Every day as winter was approaching, we'd pass by the place waiting for the weather to change and wondering when the city workers would come and fill the rink with water. Then, as winter came to an end, we'd wait for the next event: the melting of the ice. Often these distracting interests made us late for school.

I recall that late one winter as the ice thawed, several boys had ventured out onto the thinning ice, making attempts to break off an ice raft they could float on. Spurred on by a double-dare, I ventured out onto the ice and began kicking holes in the ice in a circular pattern around myself. I managed to break off the piece I was standing on, and a helpful friend gave my frosty raft a nice shove, and out I went—out toward the center of the pond and away from my companions. Initially I enjoyed the cheers of my friends for my heroic act, but then I noticed that they were beginning to turn away for the trek toward school. My pleas for help fell on deaf ears, and there was only one thing to do: jump in and wade toward shore and get myself to school.

Later that morning, my mother showed up at school with a fresh pair of Wranglers and some dry socks. She had time for only one question: "What made you think to do something so stupid?" I said the only thing a grade school boy would naturally say in that same predicament: "All the other boys were doing it."

There's a real leadership principle here. Wisely or unwisely, we grade-school buddies banded together and trusted each other. People will follow you through some pretty crazy stuff in ministry, but there has to be a relationship built on trust. Communicating a positive direction is vital. An effective leader rarely communicates from a negative place. A wise leader will communicate a forward direction in which people will want to participate. Don't talk the church's leadership down, period. This will get you nowhere. Don't build off of the negatives of other leaders. Build your leadership on a positive forward plan. I can't tell you how many times I've heard of a senior pastor being run out of the church by his disgruntled staff or of subordinate leaders who later found themselves looking for work. History has a way of repeating itself. Church history is no different.

Confrontation is sometimes necessary, even confrontation of church leadership. This may very well mean you will pay for your godly leadership with your employment, but you must remember that part of your responsibility is to represent truth.

There are a few times when you must speak up no matter what the cost. What are those times?

First, when you've been offended by a leader's words or actions, you must speak. Do so first to that leader in private. You must tell them how their words or actions have hurt you. If you tend to avoid confrontation, you may find yourself involved in confrontation anyway because you allowed the problem to grow. It's usually better to deal with problems at the front end.

Second, when there is open sin, there must be confrontation. I would even take this a step further and say if there is even the appearance of sin, or if something is happening that will likely end in sin, a wise leader will speak up. Better to fire a shot over the bow and call attention to a dangerous pattern than to say nothing and pay for it later.

A young youth pastor I know became concerned about the interactions of one of his male youth leaders with some of the girls in the youth group. In many ways, this thirty-something guy acted more like the kids than a grown man, and this seemed to my friend to be especially true around the female students. Though there wasn't evidence that anything immoral had taken place, my friend was uncomfortable with the situation. Even though there was no obvious sin, he felt like it needed to be addressed before something did happen.

He spoke with the volunteer, laying out some guidelines for appropriate interactions with the students. All this was going on while my friend was transitioning to a new ministry in another town, so he also brought the concern to the attention of the church leadership, suggesting that they step up their oversight after he moved away. Sadly, there was no follow-through from the church leadership after my friend left. Several months later, the volunteer was arrested on molestation charges. It's always better to say something, no matter how uncomfortable it makes you. You just may avert a disaster with great consequences.

Third, when leadership causes dissension and turmoil, it can be appropriate to speak up. There is a type of leadership that stirs people up because biblical truth is being presented and it makes God's people uncomfortable. That is not what we're talking about here. I'm talking about leadership that is unbiblical or divisive in nature. Rob was an associate pastor who regularly used his leadership position to be divisive. Wishing to be the senior pastor, he would constantly encourage church members to work against the church leadership. He would look for opportunities to speak against the plans of the elders. This kind of leadership is a divisive cancer to church health.

If you are going to confront a leader, there are some things you must consider first. In Matthew 18, God has given us guidelines for confronting. These should be followed. Also, recognize before you go into confrontation that if you are dealing with an issue of sin or exposing unbiblical practices, you may pay for your action with your employment. Though that may not sound particularly comforting, I can assure that God will protect you and take care of you even if you are terminated. You may also want to seek out other godly partners to go with you as you confront a leader. This is in keeping with Matthew 18, and as Scripture says, "A cord of three strands is not quickly broken" (Ecclesiastes 4:12).

When you are facing a difficult situation with church leaders, offer leadership in your own area first. The purpose of this is not to build a following away from the church leadership but to start where you are planted. Your primary responsibility is to provide leadership in your own ministry area and to those who are under your direct care.

The principle of "leaders lead!" applies both in leading down and in leading up. I usually like to avoid language that paints a hierarchal picture of the church and its structure, but the truth is that even in churches that heavily promote a horizontal team structure, there is still some hierarchy. Every leader reports to someone, and we cannot deny that there is at least some guidance in Scripture for having leadership structures in the church. These structures may apply varying degrees of authority and oversight, but every church has some kind of leadership flowchart. (If your church doesn't have one, it might be a good idea to ask that one be drawn up for the sake of clarity.)

The ground-level challenge is to be a provider of leadership that benefits both the team or cause you lead—leading down—and also benefits those up the leadership chain in your church, however developed those structures may appear—leading up. What do I mean by this? Leading down is fairly self-explanatory: We work with and direct other leaders and staff who report to us. We oversee their ministries and their work, we mentor newer team members, and we encourage those under us through regular performance reviews and positive feedback.

Leading up is more of a challenge to understand, but it's a fact that the exercising of our leadership can benefit those above us as well. I would contend that when the spiritual gift of leadership is given, it is not given just for those who work for us but also for those to whom we are responsible. Leading up happens when we use our spiritual gifts and strengths and our connection with the church body to benefit those above us and outside of our regular leadership responsibilities.

We do this in a number of ways. We do it by simply bringing our unique perspective to the table when decisions or plans are being made. Many shotgun riders sit too quietly in larger team meetings. God has given you gifts and abilities and a connection with a particular segment of your church body. You know these people and their needs better than anyone else on staff, and they are as much participants in the body as the chairman of the church board.

We also lead up when we go out of our way to help fill needs in other areas outside of our own area. There is a teacher in our preschool program who is gifted at making bulletin boards. She can make the most beautiful boards and has used her talents to highlight some of our church's ministries. This would not be that unusual except that it's not part of her normal responsibilities as a preschool teacher to create attractive bulletin boards. As a matter of fact, this woman doesn't even attend our church! She is a true leader.

I was having lunch with a pastor friend who serves on a satellite campus of a large church in my city. I was telling Robert of a challenge we were having managing the child care during an upcoming marriage conference that is part of my responsibility. The conference had grown considerably in recent years, and the child care we provided was becoming unmanageable. Without hesitation Robert said, "Our facility is right around the corner. Why don't you let me and my people handle it?" Robert is a true leader.

Though I am not responsible to lead the youth pastor and director in our church, I like to spend time with them, encouraging and helping them in ways that I can. I'm not responsible for them or their effectiveness in any official capacity, but from time to time, they will come to me and ask a question about how to handle a particular situation. Sometimes they just need a friend to hear about the challenges they face. I find pleasure in mentoring and helping them develop as leaders, and they seem to respond to the relationship. There is not another person on our pastoral team right now who has been in their shoes like I have. I understand their struggles and their challenges, and it would be a shame to let the almost two decades I spent in their position go to waste simply because it's not in my job description.

We also lead up when we help other leaders out with their workload. If we are asked to speak up front or lead meetings in others' areas when they're sick or out of town, we use our gifts and abilities to benefit those over us.

Finally, we can lead up by helping to shape the direction of those leading above us. For instance, occasionally I will ask to speak with my senior pastor about a need I see in the congregation. A couple of years ago, I noticed that it was becoming more difficult to recruit leaders. It seemed that too many people were sitting on the sidelines who had previously served in various volunteer capacities. I mentioned this to my senior pastor, and without me even suggesting it, he began a message series on serving. The end result was that more people saw the needs and the importance of serving. For several weeks after that series, my phone rang regularly with people calling to ask if there was somewhere they could serve in our ministry—I didn't call them; they called me! One small act of leading up brought about a significant change.

There's a temptation to think that leaders up the chain don't care or don't listen, but the truth is, they generally do. Senior pastors are constantly on the lookout for preaching content and direction. Your leaders have struggles just like you and I do. It's true we could take the "it's not my job" attitude, but that's not what leaders do. Leaders lead!

No one has a better vantage point of the church and what's going on in it, and no one knows the people better than shotgun riders. Many times I've discovered that a leader up the chain was unaware of some happening in the church that to me seemed rather major—a ministry leader was in the hospital or a prominent couple in the church was going through a divorce or a new ministry had been launched. It's easy to become frustrated, thinking our superiors should know about all these things; that they should be more in touch with the people. But before you rush quickly to judgment, know that leaders on your own team may say the same thing about you, and they are concerned with things you're probably unaware of yourself! I once needed to hire a part-time staff person to fill a spot on my team. I had taken on new responsibilities, and there was growth in attendance in my area. I made several presentations to various boards and leaders. After no forward movement, I went up the chain and was granted a hearing by my senior pastor. He informed me that the church was going through a difficult financial period and that the leaders were actually holding private meetings to try to figure out how to avoid laying off staff. I had no idea that the leadership was struggling with such weighty issues. Use your vantage point in the church to serve the people, and use it to benefit those above you as well.

The supremacy of grace, shepherding first, people before programs, and leaders lead: these are the principles I live by in ministry. They guide my thinking and ministry activities. It's my prayer that if you are feeling the need for direction, these principles may give you some guidance. But the important thing is not so much that you adhere to my particular principles. The important thing is that you recognize or develop your own. As I mentioned at the beginning of this chapter, we all have something guiding us. It's important to become aware of the forces driving our day-to-day decisions and activities.

If you've never done this, take some time right now and write down a few thoughts about what is driving you in ministry. Think about the things you find yourself repeating to your staff and volunteers. As you develop your guiding principles, you will begin to see how God has wired you for your ministry, and they will help you thrive as a shotgun rider.

CHAPTER TEN

MAKE IT WORK

So you're on the shotgun ride, with all of its challenges and difficulties. It's my prayer that in these pages you have been renewed in your commitment to your post, and you have a revitalized desire to complete the work to which God has called you. The best of the ride still lies ahead!

I can't help but think of a pivotal scene in the movie *The Princess Bride*. At the most desperate moment, when all hope seems lost and Princess Buttercup is about to be forced to marry the prince she despises, we find Inigo Montoya, a key figure, slouched in a drunken stupor and nursing a bottle. He is yelling out to Vizzini in his thick Spanish accent, "I am waiting for you, Vizzini. You told me to go back to the beginning. So I have. Vizzinin *gave orders*. When the job went wrong, he went back to the beginning. Well, this is the beginning. And I'm staying till Vizzini come."

There are desperate times along the journey when it's helpful to go back to the beginning. Go back to where you first sensed the call of God on your life. If you can't make the physical journey, at least make a mental one. Review the events that convinced you to take on your post, to follow his lead. Write them down if you must, but remind yourself that you were given a holy assignment, and he will be proven faithful. My friend, if you are floundering, you will do well to remind yourself of his call on your life, because along with that call comes the strength he provides for the ride. The kind of strength needed for the shotgun ride can only be found in him.

Jesus never said it would be easy, though: he actually said the opposite.

He said they would hate us because of him, and many of us have tasted some of that hardship. Although at times we may be tempted to whine and complain about our lot, why do we expect a life of comfort and ease? Why do we cry "Unjust!" when we experience what Christ said would be part of the call?

The message here is not simply "stop crying and carry on." Our emotions are a real part of this ministry journey, and I implore you to take the honest approach when facing the pain of a ministry valley. I challenge you to make a declaration that it hurts. Sometimes it needs to be said to those who caused the wound, and yes, it sometimes needs to be said to the One who called us as a way for us to settle in with the realities of the ride.

If you have been called, then you've been summoned for a purpose. God must have seen in you some qualities that would be useful in the building of his church. Sure, we are imperfect people without special powers, but that's just the point. He chooses to use the weak things of this world to accomplish his will. You will do well to take your eyes off of the impasses in front of you. You must see that he has prepared you and called you to your post. You are exactly the person he had in mind for this assignment, and he will certainly empower you for it.

You are a called one, and this calling cannot be defined by the challenges, nor can it be defined by the voices around you. Rather, your calling is defined by the Caller, by the One who sees the end. So take your concerns to him. Present to him the challenges you face. He knows and sees and is aware of your frailty, your weaknesses, and your inabilities—and that's exactly the point. It's not about your strength but about his. Ministry success will only come when you seek him first. Like Peter out on the water, it's best to take your eyes off of your surroundings and put them on him.

Whatever the specifics of your assignment, know that somehow Jesus intends to use you in the building up of his kingdom through the making of disciples. Maybe your work seems insignificant; maybe you labor in some back office unnoticed by others. Your work, the work of the church, is to make disciples, and for this task an all-hands-on-deck mentality is required. God calls and gifts a variety of people, and all of the parts are required for the body to function best. Whatever you do, no matter how insignificant it feels, to him you are as the most important person in the most significant of roles. This is the purpose for which he created you.

We will do well to remind ourselves that the most important things we do are not things at all, but rather relationships. When you were called to complete your assignment, you were brought to a people work. Yes, there are projects, events, and schedules, but we should be ready to set all of that aside when there are people in view. It is in community that growth and discipleship happen and life change occurs. When your hands are full with your projects and one of your constituents enters the room, drop everything and put your work aside. Look that person in the eye. Listen. Put people above projects. Take note of the people under your tin roof. Look for opportunities to encourage and develop others, whatever your title is.

We must never forget that at the foundation of ministry is the idea that God extended his grace to us. He gave his life for us by providing his precious Son to die in our place so we can live. It is out of appreciation for that gift that we serve him. And it is in this service, this holy assignment, that we are reminded that he has called imperfect, sinful people to be used to build his kingdom. It is that very attitude extended to us, that selfless love for others, which we extend to those around us. Yes, grace is the vehicle by which we are saved, and we must pass grace along to others in that same spirit of grace as we love them, lead them, and build them.

As you serve, remember the importance of building trust with those on your team. Be the trustworthy one. Not simply the one who finishes assignments on time, although that is important, but the one who is trusted in a relational sense. Be a safe person with whom others are willing to drop their guard. It is only when there is trust among partners that much can be accomplished, and this requires the attention of wise shotgun riders.

You will do well to think long-term. Take care of yourself and your family. These are nonnegotiables for your journey. Your ministry effectiveness depends on it. Keep an eye on the gauges. Be sure to find strength daily with your Father. Remember that even Jesus would regularly slip away and spend time with his Father. If the Son of God himself did this, then how much more do we need to draw strength from the same source?

Finally, if you find yourself in the place of conflict, be confident that you are not alone. No matter how ugly or hurtful your situation, know that you have been called to shine a light into a dark moment. Perhaps you are finished, at a point of no return: please understand that your situation is not all about you. You may be staring into the eyes of evil itself, but you must understand that God has plans to build his church, and even the gates of hell cannot stand against that agenda. It may be that you have been called to this moment to communicate God's heart and truth into the situation. He never said it would be easy, but he did say that he would be with us even to the end of the age. So take heart, my friend. There may be difficult days ahead, but you are on assignment from the Father, and he will not let you be overcome if you trust in him and follow his lead.

A Final Thought

The summers I worked at camp during college gave me a love for the wonder of times gone by. I worked on the maintenance crew, and most of the camp vehicles and equipment, though well maintained, were discards from bygone days reclaimed from garages and farmyards across the Midwest. My favorite— all the guys' favorite—was an old truck we affectionately called Red.

Red was a burly ride made of thick, unyielding steel, not like today's trucks. She was a real workhorse, the kind of pickup that turns boys into men: a 1968 four-wheel-drive International step side with a 400-cubic-inch V8 and a Holly four-barrel carburetor. Red was a real piece of hardworking machinery. She was the pride and joy of our crew, and it made you feel important to so much as mention that you had been out for a ride. Our chests swelled each time we climbed inside, and there was almost always a momentary pause as we sat there basking in the dusty aroma of aged steel and a mixture of old grease and motor oil. Sometimes we'd catch ourselves running a hand across the dash or seat just to take in the rich history and absorb her strength—and then the key was turned.

Every ride was an adventure. What I remember most was not so much the fun of driving this powerful piece of Americana, but the desire to ride shotgun. For me, that was the favored seat: the spot where you could feel every bump and experience the adventure without the arduous labor of operating the antique.

I felt like a king riding up high in that seat—we all did. The ride was euphoric; you just couldn't help but feel it. The stiff bounce of the steel springs in the seat never seemed like an inconvenience. You actually yearned for it, anticipating each bump in the road and each shift of the stick. It was all part of the mystique of the ride, and every bounce served as a reminder of the heft of metal, the craftsmanship, and the bulk of power that was at your hands. Sometimes as we rode along with our elbows perched out the windows and the warm summer breeze wafting through, we'd look at each other, knowingly. No one ever said it, but we all knew they just didn't make 'em like Red anymore.

We used that truck for everything we could think of. We ripped stumps out of the ground and pulled loaded hay wagons; we hauled trailers weighed down with camper luggage, we moved countless loads of firewood and pulled tractors out of the mud when they got stuck. Every new challenge sent a renewed wave of exhilaration through our team of young sleeveless studs, and there wasn't one assignment that ever held Red back.

The grand privilege of riding shotgun has never left me. I've always felt this same way about my role in the church. Yes, there are perils, and sometimes her ways seem antiquated, but the joy of the ride outweighs it all. These are the golden years, this is the ride of my life, and I can't wait to see what's around the next corner.

You may not be the driver, the one who sets the major direction of your church. The shotgun rider never is. If you are in a large church you may not have much to do with the direction of the church at all, but you certainly have a substantial role and influence over her—way more than you know. The big picture of the church comes together in a thousand little conversations in the hallways, the kitchens, and the youth rooms of your church. Her success is largely the sum of the actions of the shotgun riders, of the way you carry out each responsibility and each assignment. The success of your church is wrapped up in the totality of the ways in which you handle each criticism and frustration. These are the interactions where parishioners, sinners, and parishioners who are sinners find the love of Christ. These are the places where vital church life and health are built.

I've spent half a pastoral career as a shotgun rider. I've seen the best and worst of church life, and still I love the ride. I'm thrilled beyond measure, and humbled, that a holy God would allow me to climb in for the ride—to have any part at all in what he is doing in his kingdom and in people's lives. Yes, there have been a lot of frustrating times along the way. Yes, there have been times I've considered leaving the ministry. But he always draws me back, back to my calling and to my love for his work. All in all there's nowhere I'd rather be right now than in this seat. So if you get one thing from this book, get this: You can and will make a difference as you faithfully follow the call of the ride. You will, in time, leave behind a legacy of lasting worth. For you, my friend, are the shotgun rider.

Please visit:
www.kdouglasbrown.com

CPSIA information can be obtained at www.ICGtesting.com
Printed in the USA
LVOW06s0920050415

433340LV00001B/1/P